From
London to Land's End.

by
DANIEL DEFOE.

and

Two Letters from the "Journey through England by a Gentleman."

First Published In
1888.

# INTRODUCTION.

At the end of this book there are a couple of letters from a volume of the "Travels in England" which were not by Defoe, although resembling Defoe's work so much in form and title, and so near to it in date of publication, that a volume of one book is often found taking the place of a volume of the other. A purchaser of Defoe's "Travels in England" has therefore to take care that he is not buying one of the mixed sets. Each of the two works describes England at the end of the first quarter of the eighteenth century. Our added descriptions of Bath, and of the journey by Chester to Holyhead, were published in 1722; Defoe's "Journey from London to the Land's End" was published in 1724, and both writers help us to compare the past with the present by their accounts of England as it was in the days of George the First, more than a hundred and sixty years ago. The days certainly are gone when, after a good haul of pilchards, seventeen can be bought for a halfpenny, and two gentlemen and their servant can have them broiled at a tavern and dine on them for three farthings, dressing and all. In another of his journeys Defoe gives a seaside tavern bill, in which the charges were ridiculously small for everything except for bread. It was war time, and the bread was the most costly item in the bill.

In the earlier part of this account of the "Journey from London to the Land's End," there is interest in the fresh memories of the rebuilding and planting at Hampton Court by William III. and Queen Mary. The passing away, and in opinion of that day the surpassing, of Wolsey's palace there were none then to regret.

A more characteristic feature in this letter will be found in the details of a project which Defoe says he had himself advocated before the Lord-Treasurer Godolphin, for the settlement of poor refugees from the Palatinate upon land in the New Forest. Our friendly relations with the Palatinate had begun with the marriage of James the First's eldest daughter to the Elector Palatine, who brought on himself much trouble by accepting the crown of Bohemia from the subjects of the Emperor Ferdinand the Second. As a Protestant Prince allied by marriage to England, he drew from England sympathies and ineffectual assistance. Many years afterwards, during the war with France in Queen Anne's time, the allies were unprosperous in 1707, and Marshal Villars was victorious upon the Rhine. The pressure of public feeling on behalf of refugees from the Palatinate did not last long enough for any action to be taken. But if it had seemed well to the Government to accept the project advocated by Defoe, we should have had a clearance of what is now the most beautiful part of the New Forest, near Lyndhurst; and in place of the little area that still preserves all the best features of forest land, we should have had a town of Englishmen descended from the latest of the German settlements upon our soil. Upon the political economy of Defoe's project, and the accuracy of his calculations, and the more or less resemblance of his scheme to the system of free grants of land in unsettled regions beyond the sea, each reader will speculate in his own way.

There are interesting notes on the extent of the sheep farming upon the Downs crossed in this journey. There is high praise of the ladies of Dorsetshire. There are some pleasant notes upon dialect, including the story, often quoted, of the schoolboy whom Defoe saw and heard reading his Bible in class, and while following every word and line with his eye, translating it as he went into his own way of speech. Thus he turned the third verse of the fifth chapter of Solomon's Song, "I have put off my coat; how shall I put it on? I have washed my feet; how shall I defile them?" into "Chav a doffed my cooat; how shall I don't? Chav a washed my veet; how shall I moil 'em?" This is a good example of intelligent reading; for the boy took in the sense of the printed lines, and then made it his own by giving homely utterance to what he understood.

Defoe tells in this letter several tales of the shorefolk about the Great Storm of November, 1703, recollection of which Addison used effectively in the following year in his poem on the Battle of Blenheim. There was the sweeping away of the first Eddystone Lighthouse, with the builder, confident in its strength, who had desired to be in it some night when the wind blew with unusual fury. There was the story also of the man and two boys, in a ship laden with tin, blown out of Helford Haven, and of their hairbreadth escape by counsel of one of the boys who ran the ship through rocks into a narrow creek that he knew in the Isle of Wight. The form of the coast has been changed so much since 1703 by the beat of many storms, that it may be now impossible to know that little cove as the boy knew it. It must have been at the back of the island. Were the storm waves tossing then in Steephill Cove or Luccombe Chine? Does there survive anywhere a tradition of that perilous landing? Probably not. Wreck follows upon wreck, and memory of many tales of death and peril on the rock-bound coast lie between us and the boy who took the helm when he spied the well-known creek as the great storm was sweeping the ship on to destruction. From the next year after that famous storm, Defoe gives a memory of disaster seen by himself at Plymouth in the wreck of a little fleet from Barbadoes. In another part of this letter he tells what he had seen of a fight at sea between three French men-of-war and two English with a convoy of two or three trading vessels.

There will be found also in this letter a good story of a Cornish dog taken from Carew's "Survey of Cornwall," which may pair with that of the London dog who lately took a wounded fellow dog to hospital.

The writer of this letter speaks of the civil war times as a friend of monarchy, but when he tells of the landing of William III. at Torbay, he suggests that the people had good reason for rejoicing, and throughout the journey he takes note of a great inequality he finds in distribution of the right of returning members to Parliament. It is evident that he could propound a project for a Reform Bill, though he is careful so to describe England as to avoid giving offence to Englishmen of any party. The possibility of some change for the better here and there presents itself; Defoe glances and passes on. His theme is England and the English; he shows us, clearly and very simply, what he has seen of the social life and manners of the people, of the features of the land itself, and their relation to its industries; traces of the past, and prospects of the future; shepherds, fishermen, merchants; catching of salmon peel in mill-weirs, and catching of husbands at provincial assemblies; with whatever else he found worth friendly observation.

H. M.

# FROM LONDON TO LAND'S END

Sir,

I find so much left to speak of, and so many things to say in every part of England, that my journey cannot be barren of intelligence which way soever I turn; no, though I were to oblige myself to say nothing of anything that had been spoken of before.

I intended once to have gone due west this journey; but then I should have been obliged to crowd my observations so close (to bring Hampton Court, Windsor, Blenheim, Oxford, the Bath and Bristol all into one letter; all those remarkable places lying in a line, as it were, in one point of the compass) as to have made my letter too long, or my observations too light and superficial, as others have done before me.

This letter will divide the weighty task, and consequently make it sit lighter on the memory, be pleasanter to the reader, and make my progress the more regular: I shall therefore take in Hampton Court and Windsor in this journey; the first at my setting out, and the last at my return, and the rest as their situation demands.

As I came down from Kingston, in my last circuit, by the south bank of the Thames, on the Surrey side of the river; so I go up to Hampton Court now on the north bank, and on the Middlesex side, which I mention, because, as the sides of the country bordering on the river lie parallel, so the beauty of the country, the pleasant situations, the glory of innumerable fine buildings (noblemen's and gentlemen's houses, and citizens' retreats), are so equal a match to what I had described on the other side that one knows not which to give the preference to: but as I must speak of them again, when I come to write of the county of Middlesex, which I have now purposely omitted; so I pass them over here, except the palace of Hampton only, which I mentioned in "Middlesex," for the reasons above.

Hampton Court lies on the north bank of the River Thames, about two small miles from Kingston, and on the road from Staines to Kingston Bridge; so that the road straightening the parks a little, they were obliged to part the parks, and leave the Paddock and the great park part on the other side the road—a testimony of that just regard that the kings of England always had, and still have, to the common good, and to the service of the country, that they would not interrupt the course of the road, or cause the poor people to go out of the way of their business to or from the markets and fairs, for any pleasure of their own whatsoever.

The palace of Hampton Court was first founded and built from the ground by that great statesman and favourite of King Henry VIII, Cardinal Wolsey; and if it be a just observation anywhere, as is made from the situation of the old abbeys and monasteries, the clergy were excellent judges of the beauty and pleasantness of the country, and chose always to plant in the best; I say, if it was a just observation in any case, it was in this; for if there be a situation on the whole river between Staines Bridge and Windsor Bridge pleasanter than another, it is this of Hampton; close to the river, yet not offended by the rising of its waters in floods or storms; near to the reflux of the tides, but not quite so near as to be affected with any foulness of the water which the flowing of the tides generally is the occasion of. The gardens extend almost to the bank of the river, yet are never overflowed; nor are there any marshes on either side the river to make the waters stagnate, or the air unwholesome on that account. The river is high enough to be navigable, and low enough to be a little pleasantly rapid; so that the stream looks always cheerful, not slow and sleeping, like a pond. This keeps the waters always clear and clean, the bottom in view, the fish playing and in sight; and, in a word, it has everything that can make an inland (or, as I may call it, a country) river pleasant and agreeable.

I shall sing you no songs here of the river in the first person of a water-nymph, a goddess, and I know not what, according to the humour of the ancient poets; I shall talk nothing of the marriage of old Isis, the male river, with the beautiful Thame, the female river (a whimsey as simple as the subject was empty); but I shall speak of the river as occasion presents, as it really is made glorious by the splendour of its shores, gilded with noble palaces, strong fortifications, large hospitals, and public buildings; with the greatest bridge, and the greatest city in the world, made famous by the opulence of its merchants, the increase and extensiveness of its commerce; by its invincible navies, and by the innumerable fleets of ships sailing upon it to and from all parts of the world.

As I meet with the river upwards in my travels through the inland country I shall speak of it, as it is the channel for conveying an infinite quantity of provisions from remote counties to London, and enriching all the counties again that lie near it by the return of wealth and trade from the city; and in describing these things I expect both to inform and divert my readers, and speak in a more masculine manner, more to the dignity of the subject, and also more to their satisfaction, than I could do any other way.

There is little more to be said of the Thames relating to Hampton Court, than that it adds by its neighbourhood to the pleasure of the situation; for as to passing by water to and from London, though in summer it is exceeding pleasant, yet the passage is a little too long to make it easy to the ladies, especially to be crowded up in the small boats which usually go upon the Thames for pleasure.

The prince and princess, indeed, I remember came once down by water upon the occasion of her Royal Highness's being great with child, and near her time—so near that she was delivered within two or three days after. But this passage being in the royal barges, with strength of oars, and the day exceeding fine, the passage, I say, was made very pleasant, and still the more so for being short. Again, this passage is all the way with the stream, whereas in the common passage upwards great part of the way is against the stream, which is slow and heavy.

But be the going and coming how it will by water, it is an exceeding pleasant passage by land, whether we go by the Surrey side or the Middlesex side of the water, of which I shall say more in its place.

The situation of Hampton Court being thus mentioned, and its founder, it is to be mentioned next that it fell to the Crown in the forfeiture of his Eminence the Cardinal, when the king seized his effects and estate, by which this and Whitehall (another house of his own building also) came to King Henry VIII. Two palaces fit for the kings of England, erected by one cardinal, are standing monuments of the excessive pride as well as the immense wealth of that prelate, who knew no bounds of his insolence and ambition till he was overthrown at once by the displeasure of his master.

Whoever knew Hampton Court before it was begun to be rebuilt, or altered, by the late King William, must acknowledge it was a very complete palace before, and fit for a king; and though it might not, according to the modern method of building or of gardening, pass for a thing exquisitely fine, yet it had this remaining to itself, and perhaps peculiar—namely, that it showed a situation exceedingly capable of improvement, and of being made one of the most delightful palaces in Europe.

This her Majesty Queen Mary was so sensible of, that, while the king had ordered the pulling down the old apartments, and building it up in that most beautiful form which we see them now appear in, her Majesty, impatient of enjoying so agreeable a retreat, fixed upon a building formerly made use of chiefly for landing from the river, and therefore called the Water Galley, and here, as if she had been conscious that she had but a few years to enjoy it, she ordered all the little neat curious things to be done which suited her own conveniences, and made it the pleasantest little thing within doors that could possibly be made, though its situation being such as it could not be allowed to stand after the great building was finished, we now see no remains of it.

The queen had here her gallery of beauties, being the pictures at full-length of the principal ladies attending upon her Majesty, or who were frequently in her retinue; and this was the more beautiful sight because the originals were all in being, and often to be compared with their pictures. Her Majesty had here a fine apartment, with a set of lodgings for her private retreat only, but most exquisitely furnished, particularly a fine chintz bed, then a great curiosity; another of her own work while in Holland, very magnificent, and several others; and here was also her Majesty's fine collection of Delft ware, which indeed was very large and fine; and here was also a vast stock of fine china ware, the like whereof was not then to be seen in England; the long gallery, as above, was filled with this china, and every other place where it could be placed with advantage.

The queen had here also a small bathing-room, made very fine, suited either to hot or cold bathing, as the season should invite; also a dairy, with all its conveniences, in which her Majesty took great delight. All these things were finished with expedition, that here their Majesties might repose while they saw the main building go forward. While this was doing, the gardens were laid out, the plan of them devised by the king himself, and especially the amendments and alterations were made by the king or the queen's particular special command, or by both, for their Majesties agreed so well in their fancy, and had both so good judgment in the just proportions of things, which are the principal beauties of a garden, that it may be said they both ordered everything that was done.

Here the fine parcel of limes which form the semicircle on the south front of the house by the iron gates, looking into the park, were by the dexterous hand of the head gardener removed, after some of them had been almost thirty years planted in other places, though not far off. I know the King of France in the decoration of the gardens of Versailles had oaks removed, which by their dimensions must have been above an hundred years old, and yet were taken up with so much art, and by the strength of such engines, by which such a monstrous quantity of earth was raised with them, that the trees could not feel their remove—that is to say, their growth was not at all hindered. This, I confess, makes the wonder much the less in those trees at Hampton Court gardens; but the performance was not the less difficult or nice, however, in these, and they thrive perfectly well.

While the gardens were thus laid out, the king also directed the laying the pipes for the fountains and jet-d'eaux, and particularly the dimensions of them, and what quantity of water they should cast up, and increased the number of them after the first design.

The ground on the side of the other front has received some alterations since the taking down the Water Galley; but not that part immediately next the lodgings. The orange-trees and fine Dutch bays are placed within the arches of the building under the first floor; so that the lower part of the house was all one as a greenhouse for sometime. Here stand advanced, on two pedestals of stone, two marble vases or flower-pots of most exquisite workmanship—the one done by an Englishman, and the other by a German. It is hard to say which is the best performance, though the doing of it was a kind of trial of skill between them; but it gives us room, without any partiality, to say they were both masters of their art.

The parterre on that side descends from the terrace-walk by steps, and on the left a terrace goes down to the water-side, from which the garden on the eastward front is overlooked, and gives a most pleasant prospect.

The fine scrolls and bordure of these gardens were at first edged with box, but on the queen's disliking the smell those edgings were taken up, but have since been planted again—at least, in many places—nothing making so fair and regular an edging as box, or is so soon brought to its perfection.

On the north side of the house, where the gardens seemed to want screening from the weather or the view of the chapel, and some part of the old building required to be covered from the eye, the vacant ground, which was large, is very happily cast into a wilderness, with a labyrinth and espaliers so high that they effectually take off all that part of the old building which would have been offensive to the sight. This labyrinth and wilderness is not only well designed, and completely finished, but is perfectly well kept, and the espaliers filled exactly at bottom, to the very ground, and are led up to proportioned heights on the top, so that nothing of that kind can be more beautiful.

The house itself is every way answerable on the outside to the beautiful prospect, and the two fronts are the largest and, beyond comparison, the finest of the kind in England. The great stairs go up from the second court of the palace on the right hand, and lead you to the south prospect.

I hinted in my last that King William brought into England the love of fine paintings as well as that of fine gardens; and you have an example of it in the cartoons, as they are called, being five pieces of such paintings as, if you will believe men of nice judgment and great travelling, are not to be matched in Europe. The stories are known, but especially two of them—viz., that of St. Paul preaching on Mars Hill to the self-wise Athenians, and that of St. Peter passing sentence of death on Ananias—I say, these two strike the mind with the utmost surprise, the passions are so drawn to the life; astonishment, terror, and death in the face of Ananias, zeal and a sacred fire in the eyes of the blessed Apostle, fright and surprise upon the countenances of the beholders in the piece of Ananias; all these describe themselves so naturally that you cannot but seem to discover something of the like passions, even in seeing them.

In the other there is the boldness and courage with which St. Paul undertook to talk to a set of men who, he knew, despised all the world, as thinking themselves able to teach them anything. In the audience there is anticipating pride and conceit in some, a smile or fleer of contempt in others, but a kind of sensible conviction, though crushed in its beginning, on the faces of the rest; and all together appear confounded, but have little to say, and know nothing at all of it; they gravely put him off to hear him another time; all these are seen here in the very dress of the face — that is, the very countenances which they hold while they listen to the new doctrine which the Apostle preached to a people at that time ignorant of it.

The other of the cartoons are exceeding fine but I mention these as the particular two which are most lively, which strike the fancy the soonest at first view. It is reported, but with what truth I know not, that the late French king offered an hundred thousand louis d'ors for these pictures; but this, I say, is but a report. The king brought a great many other fine pieces to England, and with them the love of fine paintings so universally spread itself among the nobility and persons of figure all over the kingdom that it is incredible what collections have been made by English gentlemen since that time, and how all Europe has been rummaged, as we may say, for pictures to bring over hither, where for twenty years they yielded the purchasers, such as collected them for sale, immense profit. But the rates are abated since that, and we begin to be glutted with the copies and frauds of the Dutch and Flemish painters who have imposed grossly upon us. But to return to the palace of Hampton Court. Queen Mary lived not to see it completely finished, and her death, with the other difficulties of that reign, put a stop to the works for some time till the king, reviving his good liking of the place, set them to work again, and it was finished as we see it. But I have been assured that had the peace continued, and the king lived to enjoy the continuance of it, his Majesty had resolved to have pulled down all the remains of the old building (such as the chapel and the large court within the first gate), and to have built up the whole palace after the manner of those two fronts already done. In these would have been an entire set of rooms of state for the receiving and, if need had been, lodging and entertaining any foreign prince with his retinue; also offices for all the Secretaries of State, Lords of the Treasury, and of Trade, to have repaired to for the despatch of such business as it might be necessary to have done there upon the king's longer residence there than ordinary; as also apartments for all the great officers of the Household; so that had the house had two great squares added, as was designed, there would have been no room to spare, or that would not have been very well filled. But the king's death put an end to all these things.

Since the death of King William, Hampton Court seemed abandoned of its patron. They have gotten a kind of proverbial saying relating to Hampton Court, viz., that it has been generally chosen by every other prince since it became a house of note. King Charles was the first that delighted in it since Queen Elizabeth's time. As for the reigns before, it was but newly forfeited to the Crown, and was not made a royal house till King Charles I., who was not only a prince that delighted in country retirements, but knew how to make choice of them by the beauty of their situation, the goodness of the air, &c. He took great delight here, and, had he lived to enjoy it in peace, had purposed to make it another thing than it was. But we all know what took him off from that felicity, and all others; and this house was at last made one of his prisons by his rebellious subjects.

His son, King Charles II., may well be said to have an aversion to the place, for the reason just mentioned—namely, the treatment his royal father met with there—and particularly that the rebel and murderer of his father, Cromwell, afterwards possessed this palace, and revelled here in the blood of the royal party, as he had done in that of his sovereign. King Charles II. therefore chose Windsor, and bestowed a vast sum in beautifying the castle there, and which brought it to the perfection we see it in at this day—some few alterations excepted, done in the time of King William.

King William (for King James is not to be named as to his choice of retired palaces, his delight running quite another way)—I say, King William fixed upon Hampton Court, and it was in his reign that Hampton Court put on new clothes, and, being dressed gay and glorious, made the figure we now see it in.

The late queen, taken up for part of her reign in her kind regards to the prince her spouse, was obliged to reside where her care of his health confined her, and in this case kept for the most part at Kensington, where he died; but her Majesty always discovered her delight to be at Windsor, where she chose the little house, as it was called, opposite to the Castle, and took the air in her chaise in the parks and forest as she saw occasion.

Now Hampton Court, by the like alternative, is come into request again; and we find his present Majesty, who is a good judge too of the pleasantness and situation of a place of that kind, has taken Hampton Court into his favour, and has made it much his choice for the summer's retreat of the Court, and where they may best enjoy the diversions of the season. When Hampton Court will find such another favourable juncture as in King William's time, when the remainder of her ashes shall be swept away, and her complete fabric, as designed by King William, shall be finished, I cannot tell; but if ever that shall be, I know no palace in Europe, Versailles excepted, which can come up to her, either for beauty and magnificence, or for extent of building, and the ornaments attending it.

From Hampton Court I directed my course for a journey into the south-west part of England; and to take up my beginning where I concluded my last, I crossed to Chertsey on the Thames, a town I mentioned before; from whence, crossing the Black Desert, as I called it, of Bagshot Heath, I directed my course for Hampshire or Hantshire, and particularly for Basingstoke—that is to say, that a little before, I passed into the great Western Road upon the heath, somewhat west of Bagshot, at a village called Blackwater, and entered Hampshire, near Hartleroe.

Before we reach Basingstoke, we get rid of that unpleasant country which I so often call a desert, and enter into a pleasant fertile country, enclosed and cultivated like the rest of England; and passing a village or two we enter Basingstoke, in the midst of woods and pastures, rich and fertile, and the country accordingly spread with the houses of the nobility and gentry, as in other places. On the right hand, a little before we come to the town, we pass at a small distance the famous fortress, so it was then, of Basing, being a house belonging then to the Marquis of Winchester, the great ancestor of the present family of the Dukes of Bolton.

This house, garrisoned by a resolute band of old soldiers, was a great curb to the rebels of the Parliament party almost through that whole war; till it was, after a vigorous defence, yielded to the conquerors by the inevitable fate of things at that time. The old house is, indeed, demolished but the successor of the family, the first Duke of Bolton, has erected a very noble fabric in the same place, or near it, which, however, is not equal to the magnificence which fame gives to the ancient house, whose strength of building only, besides the outworks, withstood the battery of cannon in several attacks, and repulsed the Roundheads three or four times when they attempted to besiege it. It is incredible what booty the garrison of this place picked up, lying as they did just on the great Western Road, where they intercepted the carriers, plundered the waggons, and suffered nothing to pass—to the great interruption of the trade of the city of London.

Basingstoke is a large populous market-town, has a good market for corn, and lately within a very few years is fallen into a manufacture, viz., of making druggets and shalloons, and such slight goods, which, however, employs a good number of the poor people, and enables them to get their bread, which knew not how to get it before.

From hence the great Western Road goes on to Whitchurch and Andover, two market-towns, and sending members to Parliament; at the last of which the Downs, or open country, begins, which we in general, though falsely, call Salisbury Plain. But my resolution being to take in my view what I had passed by before, I was obliged to go off to the left hand, to Alresford and Winchester.

Alresford was a flourishing market-town, and remarkable for this—that though it had no great trade, and particularly very little, if any, manufactures, yet there was no collection in the town for the poor, nor any poor low enough to take alms of the parish, which is what I do not think can be said of any town in England besides.

But this happy circumstance, which so distinguished Alresford from all her neighbours, was brought to an end in the year ---, when by a sudden and surprising fire the whole town, with both the church and the market-house, was reduced to a heap of rubbish; and, except a few poor huts at the remotest ends of the town, not a house left standing. The town is since that very handsomely rebuilt, and the neighbouring gentlemen contributed largely to the relief of the people, especially by sending in timber towards their building; also their market-house is handsomely built, but the church not yet, though we hear there is a fund raising likewise for that.

Here is a very large pond, or lake of water, kept up to a head by a strong batter d'eau, or dam, which the people tell us was made by the Romans; and that it is to this day part of the great Roman highway which leads from Winchester to Alton, and, as it is supposed, went on to London, though we nowhere see any remains of it, except between Winchester and Alton, and chiefly between this town and Alton.

Near this town, a little north-west, the Duke of Bolton has another seat, which, though not large, is a very handsome beautiful palace, and the gardens not only very exact, but very finely situate, the prospect and vistas noble and great, and the whole very well kept.

From hence, at the end of seven miles over the Downs, we come to the very ancient city of Winchester; not only the great church (which is so famous all over Europe, and has been so much talked of), but even the whole city has at a distance the face of venerable, and looks ancient afar off; and yet here are many modern buildings too, and some very handsome; as the college schools, with the bishop's palace, built by Bishop Morley since the late wars —the old palace of the bishop having been ruined by that known church incendiary Sir William Waller and his crew of plunderers, who, if my information is not wrong, as I believe it is not, destroyed more monuments of the dead, and defaced more churches, than all the Roundheads in England beside.

This church, and the schools also are accurately described by several writers, especially by the "Monasticon," where their antiquity and original is fully set forth. The outside of the church is as plain and coarse as if the founders had abhorred ornaments, or that William of Wickham had been a Quaker, or at least a Quietist. There is neither statue, nor a niche for a statue, to be seen on all the outside; no carved work, no spires, towers, pinnacles, balustrades, or anything; but mere walls, buttresses, windows, and coigns necessary to the support and order of the building. It has no steeple, but a short tower covered flat, as if the top of it had fallen down, and it had been covered in haste to keep the rain out till they had time to build it up again.

But the inside of the church has many very good things in it, and worth observation; it was for some ages the burying-place of the English Saxon kings, whose reliques, at the repair of the church, were collected by Bishop Fox, and being put together into large wooden chests lined with lead were again interred at the foot of the great wall in the choir, three on one side, and three on the other, with an account whose bones are in each chest. Whether the division of the reliques might be depended upon, has been doubted, but is not thought material, so that we do but believe they are all there.

The choir of the church appears very magnificent; the roof is very high, and the Gothic work in the arched part is very fine, though very old; the painting in the windows is admirably good, and easy to be distinguished by those that understand those things: the steps ascending to the choir make a very fine show, having the statues of King James and his son King Charles, in copper, finely cast; the first on the right hand, and the other on the left, as you go up to the choir.

The choir is said to be the longest in England; and as the number of prebendaries, canons, &c., are many, it required such a length. The ornaments of the choir are the effects of the bounty of several bishops. The fine altar (the noblest in England by much) was done by Bishop Morley; the roof and the coat-of-arms of the Saxon and Norman kings were done by Bishop Fox; and the fine throne for the bishop in the choir was given by Bishop Mew in his lifetime; and it was well it was for if he had ordered it by will, there is reason to believe it had never been done—that reverend prelate, notwithstanding he enjoyed so rich a bishopric, scarce leaving money enough behind him to pay for his coffin.

There are a great many persons of rank buried in this church, besides the Saxon kings mentioned above, and besides several of the most eminent bishops of the See. Just under the altar lies a son of William the Conqueror, without any monument; and behind the altar, under a very fine and venerable monument, lies the famous Lord Treasurer Weston, late Earl of Portland, Lord High Treasurer of England under King Charles I. His effigy is in copper armour at full-length, with his head raised on three cushions of the same, and is a very magnificent work. There is also a very fine monument of Cardinal Beaufort in his cardinal's robes and hat.

The monument of Sir John Cloberry is extraordinary, but more because it puts strangers upon inquiring into his story than for anything wonderful in the figure, it being cut in a modern dress (the habit gentlemen wore in those times, which, being now so much out of fashion, appears mean enough). But this gentleman's story is particular, being the person solely entrusted with the secret of the restoration of King Charles II., as the messenger that passed between General Monk on one hand, and Mr. Montague and others entrusted by King Charles II. on the other hand; which he managed so faithfully as to effect that memorable event, to which England owes the felicity of all her happy days since that time; by which faithful service Sir John Cloberry, then a private musketeer only, raised himself to the honour of a knight, with the reward of a good estate from the bounty of the king.

Everybody that goes into this church, and reads what is to be read there, will be told that the body of the church was built by the famous William of Wickham; whose monument, intimating his fame, lies in the middle of that part which was built at his expense.

He was a courtier before a bishop; and, though he had no great share of learning, he was a great promoter of it, and a lover of learned men. His natural genius was much beyond his acquired parts, and his skill in politics beyond his ecclesiastic knowledge. He is said to have put his master, King Edward III., to whom he was Secretary of State, upon the two great projects which made his reign so glorious, viz.:—First, upon setting up his claim to the crown of France, and pushing that claim by force of arms, which brought on the war with France, in which that prince was three times victorious in battle. (2) Upon setting up, or instituting the Order of the Garter; in which he (being before that made Bishop of Winchester) obtained the honour for the Bishops of Winchester of being always prelates of the Order, as an appendix to the bishopric; and he himself was the first prelate of the Order, and the ensigns of that honour are joined with his episcopal ornaments in the robing of his effigy on the monument above.

To the honour of this bishop, there are other foundations of his, as much to his fame as that of this church, of which I shall speak in their order; but particularly the college in this city, which is a noble foundation indeed. The building consists of two large courts, in which are the lodgings for the masters and scholars, and in the centre a very noble chapel; beyond that, in the second court, are the schools, with a large cloister beyond them, and some enclosures laid open for the diversion of the scholars. There also is a great hall, where the scholars dine. The funds for the support of this college are very considerable; the masters live in a very good figure, and their maintenance is sufficient to support it. They have all separate dwellings in the house, and all possible conveniences appointed them.

The scholars have exhibitions at a certain time of continuance here, if they please to study in the new college at Oxford, built by the same noble benefactor, of which I shall speak in its order.

The clergy here live at large, and very handsomely, in the Close belonging to the cathedral; where, besides the bishop's palace mentioned above, are very good houses, and very handsomely built, for the prebendaries, canons, and other dignitaries of this church. The Deanery is a very pleasant dwelling, the gardens very large, and the river running through them; but the floods in winter sometimes incommode the gardens very much.

This school has fully answered the end of the founder, who, though he was no great scholar, resolved to erect a house for the making the ages to come more learned than those that went before; and it has, I say, fully answered the end, for many learned and great men have been raised here, some of whom we shall have occasion to mention as we go on.

Among the many private inscriptions in this church, we found one made by Dr. Over, once an eminent physician in this city, on a mother and child, who, being his patients, died together and were buried in the same grave, and which intimate that one died of a fever, and the other of a dropsy:

"Surrepuit natum Febris, matrem abstulit Hydrops,
Igne Prior Fatis, Altera cepit Aqua."

As the city itself stands in a vale on the bank, and at the conjunction of two small rivers, so the country rising every way, but just as the course of the water keeps the valley open, you must necessarily, as you go out of the gates, go uphill every wry; but when once ascended, you come to the most charming plains and most pleasant country of that kind in England; which continues with very small intersections of rivers and valleys for above fifty miles, as shall appear in the sequel of this journey.

At the west gate of this city was anciently a castle, known to be so by the ruins more than by any extraordinary notice taken of it in history. What they say of it, that the Saxon kings kept their court here, is doubtful, and must be meant of the West Saxons only. And as to the tale of King Arthur's Round Table, which they pretend was kept here for him and his two dozen of knights (which table hangs up still, as a piece of antiquity to the tune of twelve hundred years, and has, as they pretend, the names of the said knights in Saxon characters, and yet such as no man can read), all this story I see so little ground to give the least credit to that I look upon it, and it shall please you, to be no better than a fib.

Where this castle stood, or whatever else it was (for some say there was no castle there), the late King Charles II. marked out a very noble design, which, had he lived, would certainly have made that part of the country the Newmarket of the ages to come; for the country hereabout far excels that of Newmarket Heath for all kinds of sport and diversion fit for a prince, nobody can dispute. And as the design included a noble palace (sufficient, like Windsor, for a summer residence of the whole court), it would certainly have diverted the king from his cursory journeys to Newmarket.

The plan of this house has received several alterations, and as it is never like to be finished, it is scarce worth recording the variety. The building is begun, and the front next the city carried up to the roof and covered, but the remainder is not begun. There was a street of houses designed from the gate of the palace down to the town, but it was never begun to be built; the park marked out was exceeding large, near ten miles in circumference, and ended west upon the open Downs, in view of the town of Stockbridge.

This house was afterwards settled, with a royal revenue also, as an appanage (established by Parliament) upon Prince George of Denmark for his life, in case he had out-lived the queen; but his Royal Highness dying before her Majesty, all hope of seeing this design perfected, or the house finished, is now vanished.

I cannot omit that there are several public edifices in this city and in the neighbourhood, as the hospitals and the building adjoining near the east gate; and towards the north a piece of an old monastery undemolished, and which is still preserved to the religion, being the residence of some private Roman Catholic gentlemen, where they have an oratory, and, as they say, live still according to the rules of St. Benedict. This building is called Hide House; and as they live very usefully, and to the highest degree obliging among their neighbours, they meet with no obstruction or disturbance from anybody.

Winchester is a place of no trade other than is naturally occasioned by the inhabitants of the city and neighbouring villages one with another. Here is no manufacture, no navigation; there was indeed an attempt to make the river navigable from Southampton, and it was once made practicable, but it never answered the expense so as to give encouragement to the undertakers.

Here is a great deal of good company, and abundance of gentry being in the neighbourhood, it adds to the sociableness of the place. The clergy also here are, generally speaking, very rich and very numerous.

As there is such good company, so they are gotten into that new-fashioned way of conversing by assemblies. I shall do no more than mention them here; they are pleasant and agreeable to the young peoples, and sometimes fatal to them, of which, in its place, Winchester has its share of the mirth. May it escape the ill-consequences!

The hospital on the south of this city, at a mile distant on the road to Southampton, is worth notice. It is said to be founded by King William Rufus, but was not endowed or appointed till later times by Cardinal Beaufort. Every traveller that knocks at the door of this house in his way, and asks for it, claims the relief of a piece of white bread and a cup of beer, and this donation is still continued. A quantity of good beer is set apart every day to be given away, and what is left is distributed to other poor, but none of it kept to the next day.

How the revenues of this hospital, which should maintain the master and thirty private gentlemen (whom they call Fellows, but ought to call Brothers), is now reduced to maintain only fourteen, while the master lives in a figure equal to the best gentleman in the country, would be well worth the inquiry of a proper visitor, if such can be named. It is a thing worthy of complaint when public charities, designed for the relief of the poor, are embezzled and depredated by the rich, and turned to the support of luxury and pride.

From Winchester is about twenty-five miles, and over the most charming plains that can anywhere be seen (far, in my opinion, excelling the plains of Mecca), we come to Salisbury. The vast flocks of sheep which one everywhere sees upon these Downs, and the great number of those flocks, is a sight truly worth observation; it is ordinary for these flocks to contain from three thousand to five thousand in a flock, and several private farmers hereabouts have two or three such flocks.

But it is more remarkable still how a great part of these Downs comes, by a new method of husbandry, to be not only made arable (which they never were in former days), but to bear excellent wheat, and great crops, too, though otherwise poor barren land, and never known to our ancestors to be capable of any such thing—nay, they would perhaps have laughed at any one that would have gone about to plough up the wild downs and hills where the sheep were wont to go. But experience has made the present age wiser and more skilful in husbandry; for by only folding the sheep upon the ploughed lands—those lands which otherwise are barren, and where the plough goes within three or four inches of the solid rock of chalk, are made fruitful and bear very good wheat, as well as rye and barley. I shall say more of this when I come to speak of the same practice farther in the country.

This plain country continues in length from Winchester to Salisbury (twenty-five miles), from thence to Dorchester (twenty-two miles), thence to Weymouth (six miles); so that they lie near fifty miles in length and breadth; they reach also in some places thirty-five to forty miles. They who would make any practicable guess at the number of sheep usually fed on these Downs may take it from a calculation made, as I was told, at Dorchester, that there were six hundred thousand sheep fed within six miles of that town, measuring every way round and the town in the centre.

As we passed this plain country, we saw a great many old camps, as well Roman as British, and several remains of the ancient inhabitants of this kingdom, and of their wars, battles, entrenchments, encampments, buildings, and other fortifications, which are indeed very agreeable to a traveller that has read anything of the history of the country. Old Sarum is as remarkable as any of these, where there is a double entrenchment, with a deep graff or ditch to either of them; the area about one hundred yards in diameter, taking in the whole crown of the hill, and thereby rendering the ascent very difficult. Near this there is one farm-house, which is all the remains I could see of any town in or near the place (for the encampment has no resemblance of a town), and yet this is called the borough of Old Sarum, and sends two members to Parliament. Whom those members can justly say they represent would be hard for them to answer.

Some will have it that the old city of Sorbiodunum or Salisbury stood here, and was afterwards (for I know not what reasons) removed to the low marshy grounds among the rivers, where it now stands. But as I see no authority for it other than mere tradition, I believe my share of it, and take it ad referendum.

Salisbury itself is indeed a large and pleasant city, though I do not think it at all the pleasanter for that which they boast so much of—namely, the water running through the middle of every street—or that it adds anything to the beauty of the place, but just the contrary; it keeps the streets always dirty, full of wet and filth and weeds, even in the middle of summer.

The city is placed upon the confluence of two large rivers, the Avon and the Willy, neither of them considerable rivers, but very large when joined together, and yet larger when they receive a third river (viz., the Naddir), which joins them near Clarendon Park, about three miles below the city; then, with a deep channel and a current less rapid, they run down to Christchurch, which is their port. And where they empty themselves into the sea, from that town upwards towards Salisbury they are made navigable to within two miles, and might be so quite into the city, were it not for the strength of the stream.

As the city of Winchester is a city without trade—that is to say, without any particular manufactures—so this city of Salisbury and all the county of Wilts, of which it is the capital, are full of a great variety of manufactures, and those some of the most considerable in England—namely, the clothing trade and the trade of flannels, druggets, and several other sorts of manufactures, of which in their order.

The city of Salisbury has two remarkable manufactures carried on in it, and which employ the poor of great part of the country round—namely, fine flannels, and long-cloths for the Turkey trade, called Salisbury whites. The people of Salisbury are gay and rich, and have a flourishing trade; and there is a great deal of good manners and good company among them—I mean, among the citizens, besides what is found among the gentlemen; for there are many good families in Salisbury besides the citizens.

This society has a great addition from the Close—that is to say, the circle of ground walled in adjacent to the cathedral; in which the families of the prebendaries and commons, and others of the clergy belonging to the cathedral, have their houses, as is usual in all cities, where there are cathedral churches. These are so considerable here, and the place so large, that it is (as it is called in general) like another city.

The cathedral is famous for the height of its spire, which is without exception the highest and the handsomest in England, being from the ground 410 feet, and yet the walls so exceeding thin that at the upper part of the spire, upon a view made by the late Sir Christopher Wren, the wall was found to be less than five inches thick; upon which a consultation was had whether the spire, or at least the upper part of it, should be taken down, it being supposed to have received some damage by the great storm in the year 1703; but it was resolved in the negative, and Sir Christopher ordered it to be so strengthened with bands of iron plates as has effectually secured it; and I have heard some of the best architects say it is stronger now than when it was first built.

They tell us here long stories of the great art used in laying the first foundation of this church, the ground being marshy and wet, occasioned by the channels of the rivers; that it was laid upon piles, according to some, and upon woolpacks, according to others. But this is not supposed by those who know that the whole country is one rock of chalk, even from the tops of the highest hills to the bottom of the deepest rivers.

They tell us this church was forty years a-building, and cost an immense sum of money; but it must be acknowledged that the inside of the work is not answerable in the decoration of things to the workmanship without. The painting in the choir is mean, and more like the ordinary method of common drawing-room or tavern painting than that of a church; the carving is good, but very little of it; and it is rather a fine church than finely set off.

The ordinary boast of this building (that there were as many gates as months, as many windows as days, as many marble pillars as hours in the year) is now no recommendation at all. However, the mention of it must be preserved: —

"As many days as in one year there be,
So many windows in one church we see;
As many marble pillars there appear
As there are hours throughout the fleeting year;
As many gates as moons one year do view:
Strange tale to tell, yet not more strange than true."

There are, however, some very fine monuments in this church; particularly one belonging to the noble family of Seymours, since Dukes of Somerset (and ancestors of the present flourishing family), which on a most melancholy occasion has been now lately opened again to receive the body of the late Duchess of Somerset, the happy consort for almost forty years of his Grace the present Duke, and only daughter and heiress of the ancient and noble family of Percy, Earls of Northumberland, whose great estate she brought into the family of Somerset, who now enjoy it.

With her was buried at the same time her Grace's daughter the Marchioness of Caermarthen (being married to the Marquis of Caermarthen, son and heir-apparent to the Lord of Leeds), who died for grief at the loss of the duchess her mother, and was buried with her; also her second son, the Duke Percy Somerset, who died a few months before, and had been buried in the Abbey church of Westminster, but was ordered to be removed and laid here with the ancestors of his house. And I hear his Grace designs to have a yet more magnificent monument erected in this cathedral for them, just by the other which is there already.

How the Dukes of Somerset came to quit this church for their burying-place, and be laid in Westminster Abbey, that I know not; but it is certain that the present Duke has chosen to have his family laid here with their ancestors, and to that end has caused the corpse of his son, the Lord Percy, as above, and one of his daughters, who had been buried in the Abbey, to be removed and brought down to this vault, which lies in that they call the Virgin Mary's Chapel, behind the altar. There is, as above, a noble monument for a late Duke and Duchess of Somerset in the place already, with their portraits at full-length, their heads lying upon cushions, the whole perfectly well wrought in fine polished Italian marble, and their sons kneeling by them. Those I suppose to be the father of the great Duke of Somerset, uncle to King Edward IV.; but after this the family lay in Westminster Abbey, where there is also a fine monument for that very duke who was beheaded by Edward VI., and who was the great patron of the Reformation.

Among other monuments of noble men in this cathedral they show you one that is very extraordinary, and to which there hangs a tale. There was in the reign of Philip and Mary a very unhappy murder committed by the then Lord Sturton, or Stourton, a family since extinct, but well known till within a few years in that country.

This Lord Stourton being guilty of the said murder, which also was aggravated with very bad circumstances, could not obtain the usual grace of the Crown (viz., to be beheaded), but Queen Mary positively ordered that, like a common malefactor, he should die at the gallows. After he was hanged, his friends desiring to have him buried at Salisbury, the bishop would not consent that he should be buried in the cathedral unless, as a farther mark of infamy, his friends would submit to this condition—viz., that the silken halter in which he was hanged should be hanged up over his grave in the church as a monument of his crime; which was accordingly done, and there it is to be seen to this day.

The putting this halter up here was not so wonderful to me as it was that the posterity of that lord, who remained in good rank some time after, should never prevail to have that mark of infamy taken off from the memory of their ancestor.

There are several other monuments in this cathedral, as particularly of two noblemen of ancient families in Scotland—one of the name of Hay, and one of the name of Gordon; but they give us nothing of their history, so that we must be content to say there they lie, and that is all.

The cloister, and the chapter-house adjoining to the church, are the finest here of any I have seen in England; the latter is octagon, or eight-square, and is 150 feet in its circumference; the roof bearing all upon one small marble pillar in the centre, which you may shake with your hand; and it is hardly to be imagined it can be any great support to the roof, which makes it the more curious (it is not indeed to be matched, I believe, in Europe).

From hence directing my course to the seaside in pursuit of my first design— viz., of viewing the whole coast of England—I left the great road and went down the east side of the river towards New Forest and Lymington; and here I saw the ancient house and seat of Clarendon, the mansion of the ancient family of Hide, ancestors of the great Earl of Clarendon, and from whence his lordship was honoured with that title, or the house erected into an honour in favour of his family.

But this being a large county, and full of memorable branches of antiquity and modern curiosity, I cannot quit my observations so soon. But being happily fixed, by the favour of a particular friend, at so beautiful a spot of ground as this of Clarendon Park, I made several little excursions from hence to view the northern parts of this county—a county so fruitful of wonders that, though I do not make antiquity my chief search, yet I must not pass it over entirely, where so much of it, and so well worth observation, is to be found, which would look as if I either understood not the value of the study, or expected my readers should be satisfied with a total omission of it.

I have mentioned that this county is generally a vast continued body of high chalky hills, whose tops spread themselves into fruitful and pleasant downs and plains, upon which great flocks of sheep are fed, &c. But the reader is desired to observe these hills and plains are most beautifully intersected and cut through by the course of divers pleasant and profitable rivers; in the course and near the banks of which there always is a chain of fruitful meadows and rich pastures, and those interspersed with innumerable pleasant towns, villages, and houses, and among them many of considerable magnitude. So that, while you view the downs, and think the country wild and uninhabited, yet when you come to descend into these vales you are surprised with the most pleasant and fertile country in England.

There are no less than four of these rivers, which meet all together at or near the city of Salisbury; especially the waters of three of them run through the streets of the city—the Nadder and the Willy and the Avon—and the course of these three lead us through the whole mountainous part of the county. The two first join their waters at Wilton, the shiretown, though a place of no great notice now; and these are the waters which run through the canal and the gardens of Wilton House, the seat of that ornament of nobility and learning, the Earl of Pembroke.

One cannot be said to have seen anything that a man of curiosity would think worth seeing in this county, and not have been at Wilton House; but not the beautiful building, not the ancient trophy of a great family, not the noble situation, not all the pleasures of the gardens, parks, fountains, hare-warren, or of whatever is rare either in art or nature, are equal to that yet more glorious sight of a noble princely palace constantly filled with its noble and proper inhabitants. The lord and proprietor, who is indeed a true patriarchal monarch, reigns here with an authority agreeable to all his subjects (family); and his reign is made agreeable, by his first practising the most exquisite government of himself, and then guiding all under him by the rules of honour and virtue, being also himself perfectly master of all the needful arts of family government—I mean, needful to make that government both easy and pleasant to those who are under it, and who therefore willingly, and by choice, conform to it.

Here an exalted genius is the instructor, a glorious example the guide, and a gentle well-directed hand the governor and law-giver to the whole; and the family, like a well-governed city, appears happy, flourishing, and regular, groaning under no grievance, pleased with what they enjoy, and enjoying everything which they ought to be pleased with.

Nor is the blessing of this noble resident extended to the family only, but even to all the country round, who in their degree feel the effects of the general beneficence, and where the neighbourhood (however poor) receive all the good they can expect, and are sure to have no injury or oppression.

The canal before the house lies parallel with the road, and receives into it the whole river Willy, or at least is able to do so; it may, indeed, be said that the river is made into a canal. When we come into the courtyards before the house there are several pieces of antiquity to entertain the curious, as particularly a noble column of porphyry, with a marble statue of Venus on the top of it. In Italy, and especially at Rome and Naples, we see a great variety of fine columns, and some of them of excellent workmanship and antiquity; and at some of the courts of the princes of Italy the like is seen, as especially at the court of Florence; but in England I do not remember to have seen anything like this, which, as they told me, is two-and-thirty feet high, and of excellent workmanship, and that it came last from Candia, but formerly from Alexandria. What may belong to the history of it any further, I suppose is not known—at least, they could tell me no more of it who showed it me.

On the left of the court was formerly a large grotto and curious water-works; and in a house, or shed, or part of the building, which opened with two folding-doors, like a coach-house, a large equestrian statue of one of the ancestors of the family in complete armour, as also another of a Roman Emperor in brass. But the last time I had the curiosity to see this house, I missed that part; so that I supposed they were removed.

As the present Earl of Pembroke, the lord of this fine palace, is a nobleman of great personal merit many other ways, so he is a man of learning and reading beyond most men of his lordship's high rank in this nation, if not in the world; and as his reading has made him a master of antiquity, and judge of such pieces of antiquity as he has had opportunity to meet with in his own travels and otherwise in the world, so it has given him a love of the study, and made him a collector of valuable things, as well in painting as in sculpture, and other excellences of art, as also of nature; insomuch that Wilton House is now a mere museum or a chamber of rarities, and we meet with several things there which are to be found nowhere else in the world.

As his lordship is a great collector of fine paintings, so I know no nobleman's house in England so prepared, as if built on purpose, to receive them; the largest and the finest pieces that can be imagined extant in the world might have found a place here capable to receive them. I say, they "might have found," as if they could not now, which is in part true; for at present the whole house is so completely filled that I see no room for any new piece to crowd in without displacing some other fine piece that hung there before. As for the value of the piece that might so offer to succeed the displaced, that the great judge of the whole collection, the earl himself, must determine; and as his judgment is perfectly good, the best picture would be sure to possess the place. In a word, here is without doubt the best, if not the greatest, collection of rarities and paintings that are to be seen together in any one nobleman's or gentleman's house in England. The piece of our Saviour washing His disciples' feet, which they show you in one of the first rooms you go into, must be spoken of by everybody that has any knowledge of painting, and is an admirable piece indeed.

You ascend the great staircase at the upper end of the hall, which is very large; at the foot of the staircase you have a Bacchus as large as life, done in fine Peloponnesian marble, carrying a young Bacchus on his arm, the young one eating grapes, and letting you see by his countenance that he is pleased with the taste of them. Nothing can be done finer, or more lively represent the thing intended—namely, the gust of the appetite, which if it be not a passion, it is an affection which is as much seen in the countenance, perhaps more than any other. One ought to stop every two steps of this staircase, as we go up, to contemplate the vast variety of pictures that cover the walls, and of some of the best masters in Europe; and yet this is but an introduction to what is beyond them.

When you are entered the apartments, such variety seizes you every way that you scarce know to which hand to turn yourself. First on one side you see several rooms filled with paintings as before, all so curious, and the variety such, that it is with reluctance that you can turn from them; while looking another way you are called off by a vast collection of busts and pieces of the greatest antiquity of the kind, both Greek and Romans; among these there is one of the Roman emperor Marcus Aurelius in basso-relievo. I never saw anything like what appears here, except in the chamber of rarities at Munich in Bavaria.

Passing these, you come into several large rooms, as if contrived for the reception of the beautiful guests that take them up; one of these is near seventy feet long, and the ceiling twenty-six feet high, with another adjoining of the same height and breadth, but not so long. Those together might be called the Great Gallery of Wilton, and might vie for paintings with the Gallery of Luxembourg, in the Faubourg of Paris.

These two rooms are filled with the family pieces of the house of Herbert, most of them by Lilly or Vandyke; and one in particular outdoes all that I ever met with, either at home or abroad; it is done, as was the mode of painting at that time, after the manner of a family piece of King Charles I., with his queen and children, which before the burning of Whitehall I remember to hang at the east end of the Long Gallery in the palace.

This piece fills the farther end of the great room which I just now mentioned; it contains the Earl of Montgomery, ancestor of the house of Herbert (not then Earls of Pembroke) and his lady, sitting, and as big as life; there are about them their own five sons and one daughter, and their daughter-in-law, who was daughter of the Duke of Buckingham, married to the elder Lord Herbert, their eldest son. It is enough to say of this piece, it is worth the labour of any lover of art to go five hundred miles to see it; and I am informed several gentlemen of quality have come from France almost on purpose. It would be endless to describe the whole set of the family pictures which take up this room, unless we would enter into the roof-tree of the family, and set down a genealogical line of the whole house.

After we have seen this fine range of beauties — for such, indeed, they are — far from being at an end of your surprise, you have three or four rooms still upon the same floor, filled with wonders as before. Nothing can be finer than the pictures themselves, nothing more surprising than the number of them. At length you descend the back stairs, which are in themselves large, though not like the other. However, not a hand's-breadth is left to crowd a picture in of the smallest size; and even the upper rooms, which might be called garrets, are not naked, but have some very good pieces in them.

Upon the whole, the genius of the noble collector may be seen in this glorious collection, than which, take them together, there is not a finer in any private hand in Europe, and in no hand at all in Britain, private or public.

The gardens are on the south of the house, and extend themselves beyond the river, a branch of which runs through one part of them, and still south of the gardens in the great park, which, extending beyond the vale, mounts the hill opening at the last to the great down, which is properly called, by way of distinction, Salisbury Plain, and leads from the city of Salisbury to Shaftesbury. Here also his lordship has a hare-warren, as it is called, though improperly. It has, indeed, been a sanctuary for the hares for many years; but the gentlemen complain that it mars their game, for that as soon as they put up a hare for their sport, if it be anywhere within two or three miles, away she runs for the warren, and there is an end of their pursuit; on the other hand, it makes all the countrymen turn poachers, and destroy the hares by what means they can. But this is a smaller matter, and of no great import one way or other.

From this pleasant and agreeable day's work I returned to Clarendon, and the next day took another short tour to the hills to see that celebrated piece of antiquity, the wonderful Stonehenge, being six miles from Salisbury, north, and upon the side of the River Avon, near the town of Amesbury. It is needless that I should enter here into any part of the dispute about which our learned antiquaries have so puzzled themselves that several books (and one of them in folio) have been published about it; some alleging it to be a heathen or pagan temple and altar, or place of sacrifice, as Mr. Jones; others a monument or trophy of victory; others a monument for the dead, as Mr. Aubrey, and the like. Again, some will have it be British, some Danish, some Saxon, some Roman, and some, before them all, Phoenician.

I shall suppose it, as the majority of all writers do, to be a monument for the dead, and the rather because men's bones have been frequently dug up in the ground near them. The common opinion that no man could ever count them, that a baker carried a basket of bread and laid a loaf upon every stone, and yet never could make out the same number twice, this I take as a mere country fiction, and a ridiculous one too. The reason why they cannot easily be told is that many of them lie half or part buried in the ground; and a piece here and a piece there only appearing above the grass, it cannot be known easily which belong to one stone and which to another, or which are separate stones, and which are joined underground to one another; otherwise, as to those which appear, they are easy to be told, and I have seen them told four times after one another, beginning every time at a different place, and every time they amounted to seventy-two in all; but then this was counting every piece of a stone of bulk which appeared above the surface of the earth, and was not evidently part of and adjoining to another, to be a distinct and separate body or stone by itself.

The form of this monument is not only described but delineated in most authors, and, indeed, it is hard to know the first but by the last. The figure was at first circular, and there were at least four rows or circles within one another. The main stones were placed upright, and they were joined on the top by cross-stones, laid from one to another, and fastened with vast mortises and tenons. Length of time has so decayed them that not only most of the cross-stones which lay on the top are fallen down, but many of the upright also, notwithstanding the weight of them is so prodigious great. How they came thither, or from whence (no stones of that kind being now to be found in that part of England near it) is still the mystery, for they are of such immense bulk that no engines or carriages which we have in use in this age could stir them.

Doubtless they had some method in former days in foreign countries, as well as here, to move heavier weights than we find practicable now. How else did Solomon's workmen build the battlement or additional wall to support the precipice of Mount Moriah, on which the Temple was built, which was all built of stones of Parian marble, each stone being forty cubits long and fourteen cubits broad, and eight cubits high or thick, which, reckoning each cubit at two feet and a half of our measure (as the learned agree to do), was one hundred feet long, thirty-five feet broad, and twenty feet thick?

These stones at Stonehenge, as Mr. Camden describes them, and in which others agree, were very large, though not so large—the upright stones twenty-four feet high, seven feet broad, sixteen feet round, and weigh twelve tons each; and the cross-stones on the top, which he calls coronets, were six or seven tons. But this does not seem equal; for if the cross-stones weighed six or seven tons, the others, as they appear now, were at least five or six times as big, and must weigh in proportion; and therefore I must think their judgment much nearer the case who judge the upright stones at sixteen tons or thereabouts (supposing them to stand a great way into the earth, as it is not doubted but they do), and the coronets or cross-stones at about two tons, which is very large too, and as much as their bulk can be thought to allow.

Upon the whole, we must take them as our ancestors have done—namely, for an erection or building so ancient that no history has handed down to us the original. As we find it, then, uncertain, we must leave it so. It is indeed a reverend piece of antiquity, and it is a great loss that the true history of it is not known. But since it is not, I think the making so many conjectures at the reality, when they know lots can but guess at it, and, above all, the insisting so long and warmly on their private opinions, is but amusing themselves and us with a doubt, which perhaps lies the deeper for their search into it.

The downs and plains in this part of England being so open, and the surface so little subject to alteration, there are more remains of antiquity to be seen upon them than in other places. For example, I think they tell us there are three-and-fifty ancient encampments or fortifications to be seen in this one county—some whereof are exceeding plain to be seen; some of one form, some of another; some of one nation, some of another—British, Danish, Saxon, Roman—as at Ebb Down, Burywood, Oldburgh Hill, Cummerford, Roundway Down, St. Ann's Hill, Bratton Castle, Clay Hill, Stournton Park, Whitecole Hill, Battlebury, Scrathbury, Tanesbury, Frippsbury, Southbury Hill, Amesbury, Great Bodwin, Easterley, Merdon, Aubery, Martenscil Hill, Barbury Castle, and many more.

Also the barrows, as we all agree to call them, are very many in number in this county, and very obvious, having suffered very little decay. These are large hillocks of earth cast up, as the ancients agree, by the soldiers over the bodies of their dead comrades slain in battle; several hundreds of these are to be seen, especially in the north part of this county, about Marlborough and the downs, from thence to St. Ann's Hill, and even every way the downs are full of them.

I have done with matters of antiquity for this county, unless you will admit me to mention the famous Parliament in the reign of Henry II. held at Clarendon, where I am now writing, and another intended to be held there in Richard II.'s time, but prevented by the barons, being then up in arms against the king.

Near this place, at Farlo, was the birthplace of the late Sir Stephen Fox, and where the town, sharing in his good fortune, shows several marks of his bounty, as particularly the building a new church from the foundation, and getting an Act of Parliament passed for making it parochial, it being but a chapel-of-ease before to an adjoining parish. Also Sir Stephen built and endowed an almshouse here for six poor women, with a master and a free school. The master is to be a clergyman, and to officiate in the church—that is to say, is to have the living, which, including the school, is very sufficient.

I am now to pursue my first design, and shall take the west part of Wiltshire in my return, where are several things still to be taken notice of, and some very well worth our stay. In the meantime I went on to Langborough, a fine seat of my Lord Colerain, which is very well kept, though the family, it seems, is not much in this country, having another estate and dwelling at Tottenham High Cross, near London.

**34**

From hence in my way to the seaside I came to New Forest, of which I have said something already with relation to the great extent of ground which lies waste, and in which there is so great a quantity of large timber, as I have spoken of already.

This waste and wild part of the country was, as some record, laid open and waste for a forest and for game by that violent tyrant William the Conqueror, and for which purpose he unpeopled the country, pulled down the houses, and, which was worse, the churches of several parishes or towns, and of abundance of villages, turning the poor people out of their habitations and possessions, and laying all open for his deer. The same histories likewise record that two of his own blood and posterity, and particularly his immediate successor William Rufus, lost their lives in this forest—one, viz., the said William Rufus, being shot with an arrow directed at a deer which the king and his company were hunting, and the arrow, glancing on a tree, changed his course, and struck the king full on the breast and killed him. This they relate as a just judgment of God on the cruel devastation made here by the Conqueror. Be it so or not, as Heaven pleases; but that the king was so killed is certain, and they show the tree on which the arrow glanced to this day. In King Charles II.'s time it was ordered to be surrounded with a pale; but as great part of the paling is down with age, whether the tree be really so old or not is to me a great question, the action being near seven hundred years ago.

I cannot omit to mention here a proposal made a few years ago to the late Lord Treasurer Godolphin for re-peopling this forest, which for some reasons I can be more particular in than any man now left alive, because I had the honour to draw up the scheme and argue it before that noble lord and some others who were principally concerned at that time in bringing over—or, rather, providing for when they were come over—the poor inhabitants of the Palatinate, a thing in itself commendable, but, as it was managed, made scandalous to England and miserable to those poor people.

Some persons being ordered by that noble lord above mentioned to consider of measures how the said poor people should be provided for, and whether they could be provided for or no without injury to the public, the answer was grounded upon this maxim—that the number of inhabitants is the wealth and strength of a kingdom, provided those inhabitants were such as by honest industry applied themselves to live by their labour, to whatsoever trades or employments they were brought up. In the next place, it was inquired what employments those poor people were brought up to. It was answered there were husbandmen and artificers of all sorts, upon which the proposal was as follows. New Forest, in Hampshire, was singled out to be the place:—

Here it was proposed to draw a great square line containing four thousand acres of land, marking out two large highways or roads through the centre, crossing both ways, so that there should be a thousand acres in each division, exclusive of the land contained in the said cross-roads.

Then it was proposed to since out twenty men and their families, who should be recommended as honest industrious men, expert in, or at least capable of being instructed in husbandry, curing and cultivating of land, breeding and feeding cattle, and the like. To each of these should be parcelled out, in equal distributions, two hundred acres of this land, so that the whole four thousand acres should be fully distributed to the said twenty families, for which they should have no rent to pay, and be liable to no taxes but such as provided for their own sick or poor, repairing their own roads, and the like. This exemption from rent and taxes to continue for twenty years, and then to pay each £50 a year to the queen—that is to say, to the Crown.

To each of these families, whom I would now call farmers, it was proposed to advance £200 in ready money as a stock to set them to work; to furnish them with cattle, horses, cows, hogs, &c.; and to hire and pay labourers to inclose, clear, and cure the land, which it would be supposed the first year would not be so much to their advantage as afterwards, allowing them timber out of the forest to build themselves houses and barns, sheds and offices, as they should have occasion; also for carts, waggons, ploughs, harrows, and the like necessary things: care to be taken that the men and their families went to work forthwith according to the design.

Thus twenty families would be immediately supplied and provided for, for there would be no doubt but these families, with so much land given them gratis, and so much money to work with, would live very well; but what would this do for the support of the rest, who were supposed to be, to every twenty farmers, forty or fifty families of other people (some of one trade, some of another), with women and children? To this it was answered that these twenty farmers would, by the consequence of their own settlements, provide for and employ such a proportion of others of their own people that, by thus providing for twenty families in a place, the whole number of Palatinates would have been provided for, had they been twenty thousand more in number than they were, and that without being any burden upon or injury to the people of England; on the contrary, they would have been an advantage and an addition of wealth and strength to the nation, and to the country in particular where they should be thus seated. For example: —

As soon as the land was marked out, the farmers put in possession of it, and the money given them, they should be obliged to go to work, in order to their settlement. Suppose it, then, to be in the spring of the year, when such work was most proper. First, all hands would be required to fence and part off the land, and clear it of the timber or bushes, or whatever else was upon it which required to be removed. The first thing, therefore, which the farmer would do would be to single out from the rest of their number every one three servants—that is to say, two men and a maid; less could not answer the preparations they would be obliged to make, and yet work hard themselves also. By the help of these they would, with good management, soon get so much of their land cured, fenced-off, ploughed, and sowed as should yield them a sufficiency of corn and kitchen stuff the very first year, both for horse-meat, hog-meat, food for the family, and some to carry to market, too, by which to bring in money to go farther on, as above.

At the first entrance they were to have the tents allowed them to live in, which they then had from the Tower; but as soon as leisure and conveniences admitted, every farmer was obliged to begin to build him a farm-house, which he would do gradually, some and some, as he could spare time from his other works, and money from his little stock.

In order to furnish himself with carts, waggons, ploughs, harrows, wheel-barrows, hurdles, and all such necessary utensils of husbandry, there would be an absolute necessity of wheelwrights or cartwrights, one at least to each division.

Thus, by the way, there would be employed three servants to each farmer, that makes sixty persons.

Four families of wheelwrights, one to each division—which, suppose five in a family, makes twenty persons. Suppose four head-carpenters, with each three men; and as at first all would be building together, they would to every house building have at least one labourer. Four families of carpenters, five to each family, and three servants, is thirty-two persons; one labourer to each house building is twenty persons more.

Thus here would be necessarily brought together in the very first of the work one hundred and thirty-two persons, besides the head-farmers, who at five also to each family are one hundred more; in all, two hundred and thirty-two.

For the necessary supply of these with provisions, clothes, household stuff, &c. (for all should be done among themselves), first, they must have at least four butchers with their families (twenty persons), four shoemakers with their families and each shoemaker two journeymen (for every trade would increase the number of customers to every trade). This is twenty-eight persons more.

They would then require a hatmaker, a glover, at least two ropemakers, four tailors, three weavers of woollen and three weavers of linen, two basket-makers, two common brewers, ten or twelve shop-keepers to furnish chandlery and grocery wares, and as many for drapery and mercery, over and above what they could work. This makes two-and-forty families more, each at five in a family, which, is two hundred and ten persons; all the labouring part of these must have at least two servants (the brewers more), which I cast up at forty more.

Add to these two ministers, one clerk, one sexton or grave-digger, with their families, two physicians, three apothecaries, two surgeons (less there could not be, only that for the beginning it might be said the physicians should be surgeons, and I take them so); this is forty-five persons, besides servants; so that, in short—to omit many tradesmen more who would be wanted among them—there would necessarily and voluntarily follow to these twenty families of farmers at least six hundred more of their own people.

It is no difficult thing to show that the ready money of £4,000 which the Government was to advance to those twenty farmers would employ and pay, and consequently subsist, all these numerous dependants in the works which must severally be done for them for the first year, after which the farmers would begin to receive their own money back again; for all these tradesmen must come to their own market to buy corn, flesh, milk, butter, cheese, bacon, &c., which after the first year the farmers, having no rent to pay, would have to spare sufficiently, and so take back their own money with advantage. I need not go on to mention how, by consequence provisions increasing and money circulating, this town should increase in a very little time.

It was proposed also that for the encouragement of all the handicraftsmen and labouring poor who, either as servants or as labourers for day-work, assisted the farmers or other tradesmen, they should have every man three acres of ground given them, with leave to build cottages upon the same, the allotments to be upon the waste at the end of the cross-roads where they entered the town.

In the centre of the square was laid out a circle of twelve acres of ground, to be cast into streets for inhabitants to build on as their ability would permit—all that would build to have ground gratis for twenty years, timber out of the forest, and convenient yards, gardens, and orchards allotted to every house.

In the great streets near where they cross each other was to be built a handsome market-house, with a town-hall for parish or corporation business, doing justice and the like; also shambles; and in a handsome part of the ground mentioned to be laid out for streets, as near the centre as might be, was to be ground laid out for the building a church, which every man should either contribute to the building of in money, or give every tenth day of his time to assist in labouring at the building.

I have omitted many tradesmen who would be wanted here, and would find a good livelihood among their country-folks only to get accidental work as day-men or labourers (of which such a town would constantly employ many), as also poor women for assistance in families (such as midwives, nurses, &c.).

Adjacent to the town was to be a certain quantity of common-land for the benefit of the cottages, that the poor might have a few sheep or cows, as their circumstances required; and this to be appointed at the several ends of the town.

There was a calculation made of what increase there would be, both of wealth and people, in twenty years in this town; what a vast consumption of provisions they would cause, more than the four thousand acres of land given them would produce, by which consumption and increase so much advantage would accrue to the public stock, and so many subjects be added to the many thousands of Great Britain, who in the next age would be all true-born Englishmen, and forget both the language and nation from whence they came. And it was in order to this that two ministers were appointed, one of which should officiate in English and the other in High Dutch, and withal to have them obliged by a law to teach all their children both to speak, read, and write the English language.

Upon their increase they would also want barbers and glaziers, painters also, and plumbers; a windmill or two, and the millers and their families; a fulling-mill and a cloth-worker; as also a master clothier or two for making a manufacture among them for their own wear, and for employing the women and children; a dyer or two for dyeing their manufactures; and, which above all is not to be omitted, four families at least of smiths, with every one two servants—considering that, besides all the family work which continually employs a smith, all the shoeing of horses, all the ironwork of ploughs, carts, waggons, harrows, &c., must be wrought by them. There was no allowance made for inns and ale-houses, seeing it would be frequent that those who kept public-houses of any sort would likewise have some other employment to carry on.

This was the scheme for settling the Palatinates, by which means twenty families of farmers, handsomely set up and supported, would lay a foundation, as I have said, for six or seven hundred of the rest of their people; and as the land in New Forest is undoubtedly good, and capable of improvement by such cultivation, so other wastes in England are to be found as fruitful as that; and twenty such villages might have been erected, the poor strangers maintained, and the nation evidently be bettered by it. As to the money to be advanced, which in the case of twenty such settlements, at £1,000 each, would be £80,000, two things were answered to it:—

1. That the annual rent to be received for all those lands after twenty years would abundantly pay the public for the first disburses on the scheme above, that rent being then to amount to £40,000 per annum.

2. More money than would have done this was expended, or rather thrown away, upon them here, to keep them in suspense, and afterwards starve them; sending them a-begging all over the nation, and shipping them off to perish in other countries. Where the mistake lay is none of my business to inquire.

I reserved this account for this place, because I passed in this journey over the very spot where the design was laid out—namely, near Lyndhurst, in the road from Rumsey to Lymington, whither I now directed my course.

Lymington is a little but populous seaport standing opposite to the Isle of Wight, in the narrow part of the strait which ships sometimes pass through in fair weather, called the Needles; and right against an ancient town of that island called Yarmouth, and which, in distinction from the great town of Yarmouth in Norfolk, is called South Yarmouth. This town of Lymington is chiefly noted for making fine salt, which is indeed excellent good; and from whence all these south parts of England are supplied, as well by water as by land carriage; and sometimes, though not often, they send salt to London, when, contrary winds having kept the Northern fleets back, the price at London has been very high; but this is very seldom and uncertain. Lymington sends two members to Parliament, and this and her salt trade is all I can say to her; for though she is very well situated as to the convenience of shipping I do not find they have any foreign commerce, except it be what we call smuggling and roguing; which, I may say, is the reigning commerce of all this part of the English coast, from the mouth of the Thames to the Land's End of Cornwall.

From hence there are but few towns on the sea-coast west, though there are several considerable rivers empty themselves into the sea; nor are there any harbours or seaports of any note except Poole. As for Christchurch, though it stands at the mouth of the Avon (which, as I have said, comes down from Salisbury, and brings with it all the waters of the south and east parts of Wiltshire, and receives also the Stour and Piddle, two Dorsetshire rivers which bring with them all the waters of the north part of Dorsetshire), yet it is a very inconsiderable poor place, scarce worth seeing, and less worth mentioning in this account, only that it sends two members to Parliament, which many poor towns in this part of England do, as well as that.

From hence I stepped up into the country north-west, to see the ancient town of Wimborne, or Wimborneminster; there I found nothing remarkable but the church, which is indeed a very great one, ancient, and yet very well built, with a very firm, strong, square tower, considerably high; but was, without doubt, much finer, when on the top of it stood a most exquisite spire—finer and taller, if fame lies not, than that at Salisbury, and by its situation in a plainer, flatter country visible, no question, much farther; but this most beautiful ornament was blown down by a sudden tempest of wind, as they tell us, in the year 1622.

The church remains a venerable piece of antiquity, and has in it the remains of a place once much more in request than it is now, for here are the monuments of several noble families, and in particular of one king, viz., King Etheldred, who was slain in battle by the Danes. He was a prince famed for piety and religion, and, according to the zeal of these times, was esteemed as a martyr, because, venturing his life against the Danes, who were heathens, he died fighting for his religion and his country. The inscription upon his grave is preserved, and has been carefully repaired, so as to be easily read, and is as follows:—

"In hoc loco quiescit Corpus S. Etheldredi, Regis West Saxonum, Martyris, qui Anno Dom. DCCCLXXII., xxiii Aprilis, per Manos Danorum Paganorum Occubuit."

In English thus:—

"Here rests the Body of Holy Etheldred, King of the West Saxons, and Martyr, who fell by the Hands of the Pagan Danes in the Year of our Lord 872, the 23rd of April."

Here are also the monuments of the great Marchioness of Exeter, mother of Edward Courtney, Earl of Devonshire, and last of the family of Courtneys who enjoyed that honour; as also of John de Beaufort, Duke of Somerset, and his wife, grandmother of King Henry VII., by her daughter Margaret, Countess of Richmond.

This last lady I mention because she was foundress of a very fine free school, which has since been enlarged and had a new benefactress in Queen Elizabeth, who has enlarged the stipend and annexed it to the foundation. The famous Cardinal Pole was Dean of this church before his exaltation.

Having said this of the church, I have said all that is worth naming of the town; except that the inhabitants, who are many and poor, are chiefly maintained by the manufacture of knitting stockings, which employs great part indeed of the county of Dorset, of which this is the first town eastward.

South of this town, over a sandy, wild, and barren country, we came to Poole, a considerable seaport, and indeed the most considerable in all this part of England; for here I found some ships, some merchants, and some trade; especially, here were a good number of ships fitted out every year to the Newfoundland fishing, in which the Poole men were said to have been particularly successful for many years past.

The town sits in the bottom of a great bay or inlet of the sea, which, entering at one narrow mouth, opens to a very great breadth within the entrance, and comes up to the very shore of this town; it runs also west up almost to the town of Wareham, a little below which it receives the rivers Frome and Piddle, the two principal rivers of the county.

This place is famous for the best and biggest oysters in all this part of England, which the people of Poole pretend to be famous for pickling; and they are barrelled up here, and sent not only to London, but to the West Indies, and to Spain and Italy, and other parts. It is observed more pearls are found in the Poole oysters, and larger, than in any other oysters about England.

As the entrance into this large bay is narrow, so it is made narrower by an island, called Branksey, which, lying the very month of the passage, divides it into two, and where there is an old castle, called Branksey Castle, built to defend the entrance, and this strength was very great advantage to the trade of this port in the time of the late war with France.

Wareham is a neat town and full of people, having a share of trade with Poole itself; it shows the ruins of a large town, and, it is apparent, has had eight churches, of which they have three remaining.

South of Wareham, and between the bay I have mentioned and the sea, lies a large tract of land which, being surrounded by the sea except on one side, is called an island, though it is really what should be called a peninsula. This tract of land is better inhabited than the sea-coast of this west end of Dorsetshire generally is, and the manufacture of stockings is carried on there also; it is called the Isle of Purbeck, and has in the middle of it a large market-town, called Corfe, and from the famous castle there the whole town is now called Corfe Castle; it is a corporation, sending members to Parliament.

This part of the country is eminent for vast quarries of stone, which is cut out flat, and used in London in great quantities for paving courtyards, alleys, avenues to houses, kitchens, footways on the sides of the High Streets, and the like; and is very profitable to the place, as also in the number of shipping employed in bringing it to London. There are also several rocks of very good marble, only that the veins in the stone are not black and white, as the Italian, but grey, red, and other colours.

From hence to Weymouth, which is 22 miles, we rode in view of the sea; the country is open, and in some respects pleasant, but not like the northern parts of the county, which are all fine carpet-ground, soft as velvet, and the herbage sweet as garden herbs, which makes their sheep be the best in England, if not in the world, and their wool fine to an extreme.

I cannot omit here a small adventure which was very surprising to me on this journey; passing this plain country, we came to an open piece of ground where a neighbouring gentleman had at a great expense laid out a proper piece of land for a decoy, or duck-coy, as some call it. The works were but newly done, the planting young, the ponds very large and well made; but the proper places for shelter of the fowl not covered, the trees not being grown, and men were still at work improving and enlarging and planting on the adjoining heath or common. Near the decoy-keeper's house were some places where young decoy ducks were hatched, or otherwise kept to fit them for their work. To preserve them from vermin (polecats, kites, and such like), they had set traps, as is usual in such cases, and a gibbet by it, where abundance of such creatures as were taken were hanged up for show.

While the decoy-man was busy showing the new works, he was alarmed with a great cry about this house for "Help! help!" and away he ran like the wind, guessing, as we supposed, that something was catched in the trap.

It was a good big boy, about thirteen or fourteen years old, that cried out, for coming to the place he found a great fowl caught by the leg in the trap, which yet was so strong and so outrageous that the boy going too near him, he flew at him and frighted him, bit him, and beat him with his wings, for he was too strong for the boy; as the master ran from the decoy, so another manservant ran from the house, and finding a strange creature fast in the trap, not knowing what it was, laid at him with a great stick. The creature fought him a good while, but at length he struck him an unlucky blow which quieted him; after this we all came up to see what the matter, and found a monstrous eagle caught by the leg in the trap, and killed by the fellow's cudgel, as above.

When the master came to know what it was, and that his man had killed it, he was ready to kill the fellow for his pains, for it was a noble creature indeed, and would have been worth a great deal to the man to have it shown about the country, or to have sold to any gentleman curious in such things; but the eagle was dead, and there we left it. It is probable this eagle had flown over the sea from France, either there or at the Isle of Wight, where the channel is not so wide; for we do not find that any eagles are known to breed in those parts of Britain.

From hence we turned up to Dorchester, the county town, though not the largest town in the county. Dorchester is indeed a pleasant agreeable town to live in, and where I thought the people seemed less divided into factions and parties than in other places; for though here are divisions, and the people are not all of one mind, either as to religion or politics, yet they did not seem to separate with so much animosity as in other places. Here I saw the Church of England clergyman, and the Dissenting minister or preacher drinking tea together, and conversing with civility and good neighbourhood, like Catholic Christians and men of a Catholic and extensive charity. The town is populous, though not large; the streets broad, but the buildings old and low. However, there is good company, and a good deal of it; and a man that coveted a retreat in this world might as agreeably spend his time and as well in Dorchester as in any town I know in England.

The downs round this town are exceeding pleasant, and come up on, every side, even to the very streets' end; and here it was that they told me that there were six hundred thousand sheep fed on the downs within six miles of the town—that is, six miles every way, which is twelve miles in diameter, and thirty-six miles in circumference. This, I say, I was told—I do not affirm it to be true; but when I viewed the country round, I confess I could not but incline to believe it.

It is observable of these sheep that they are exceeding fruitful, the ewes generally bringing two lambs, and they are for that reason bought by all the farmers through the east part of England, who come to Burford Fair in this country to buy them, and carry them into Kent and Surrey eastward, and into Buckinghamshire and Bedfordshire and Oxfordshire north; even our Banstead Downs in Surrey, so famed for good mutton, is supplied from this place. The grass or herbage of these downs is full of the sweetest and the most aromatic plants, such as nourish the sheep to a strange degree; and the sheep's dung, again, nourishes that herbage to a strange degree; so that the valleys are rendered extremely fruitful by the washing of the water in hasty showers from off these hills.

An eminent instance of this is seen at Amesbury, in Wiltshire, the next county to this; for it is the same thing in proportion over this whole county. I was told that at this town there was a meadow on the bank of the River Avon, which runs thence to Salisbury, which was let for £12 a year per acre for the grass only. This I inquired particularly after at the place, and was assured by the inhabitants, as one man, that the fact was true, and was showed the meadows. The grass which grew on them was such as grew to the length of ten or twelve feet, rising up to a good height and then taking root again, and was of so rich a nature as to answer very well such an extravagant rent.

The reason they gave for this was the extraordinary richness of the soil, made so, as above, by the falling or washing of the rains from the hills adjacent, by which, though no other land thereabouts had such a kind of grass, yet all other meadows and low grounds of the valley were extremely rich in proportion.

There are abundance of good families, and of very ancient lines in the neighbourhood of this town of Dorchester, as the Napiers, the Courtneys, Strangeways, Seymours, Banks, Tregonells, Sydenhams, and many others, some of which have very great estates in the county, and in particular Colonel Strangeways, Napier, and Courtney. The first of these is master of the famous swannery or nursery of swans, the like of which, I believe, is not in Europe. I wonder any man should pretend to travel over this country, and pass by it, too, and then write his account and take no notice of it.

From Dorchester it is six miles to the seaside south, and the ocean in view almost all the way. The first town you come to is Weymouth, or Weymouth and Melcombe, two towns lying at the mouth of a little rivulet which they call the Wey, but scarce claims the name of a river. However, the entrance makes a very good though small harbour, and they are joined by a wooden bridge; so that nothing but the harbour parts them; yet they are separate corporations, and choose each of them two members of Parliament, just as London and Southwark.

Weymouth is a sweet, clean, agreeable town, considering its low situation, and close to the sea; it is well built, and has a great many good substantial merchants in it who drive a considerable trade, and have a good number of ships belonging to the town. They carry on now, in time of peace, a trade with France; but, besides this, they trade also to Portugal, Spain, Newfoundland, and Virginia; and they have a large correspondence also up in the country for the consumption of their returns; especially the wine trade and the Newfoundland trade are considerable here.

Without the harbour is an old castle, called Sandfoot Castle; and over against them, where there is a good road for ships to put in on occasions of bad weather, is Portland Castle, and the road is called Portland Road. While I was here once, there came a merchant-ship into that road called Portland Road under a very hard storm of wind; she was homeward bound from Oporto for London, laden with wines; and as she came in she made signals of distress to the town, firing guns for help, and the like, as is usual in such cases; it was in the dark of the night that the ship came in, and, by the help of her own pilot, found her way into the road, where she came to an anchor, but, as I say, fired guns for help.

The venturous Weymouth men went off, even before it was light, with two boats to see who she was, and what condition she was in; and found she was come to an anchor, and had struck her topmasts; but that she had been in bad weather, had lost an anchor and cable before, and had but one cable to trust to, which did hold her, but was weak; and as the storm continued to blow, they expected every hour to go on shore and split to pieces.

Upon this the Weymouth boats came back with such diligence that in less than three hours they were on board them again with an anchor and cable, which they immediately bent in its place, and let go to assist the other, and thereby secured the ship. It is true that they took a good price of the master for the help they gave him; for they made him draw a bill on his owners at London for £12 for the use of the anchor, cable, and boat, besides some gratuities to the men. But they saved the ship and cargo by it, and in three or four days the weather was calm, and he proceeded on his voyage, returning the anchor and cable again; so that, upon the whole, it was not so extravagant as at first I thought it to be.

The Isle of Portland, on which the castle I mentioned stands, lies right against this Port of Weymouth. Hence it is that our best and whitest freestone comes, with which the Cathedral of St. Paul's, the Monument, and all the public edifices in the City of London are chiefly built; and it is wonderful, and well worth the observation of a traveller, to see the quarries in the rocks from whence they are cut out, what stones, and of what prodigious a size are cut out there.

The island is indeed little more than one continued rock of freestone, and the height of the land is such that from this island they see in clear weather above half over the Channel to France, though the Channel here is very broad. The sea off of this island, and especially to the west of it, is counted the most dangerous part of the British Channel. Due south, there is almost a continued disturbance in the waters, by reason of what they call two tides meeting, which I take to be no more than the sets of the currents from the French coast and from the English shore meeting: this they call Portland Race; and several ships, not aware of these currents, have been embayed to the west of Portland, and been driven on shore on the beach (of which I shall speak presently), and there lost.

To prevent this danger, and guide the mariner in these distresses, they have within these few months set up two lighthouses on the two points of that island; and they had not been many months set up, with the directions given to the public for their bearings, but we found three outward-bound East India ships which were in distress in the night, in a hard extreme gale of wind, were so directed by those lights that they avoided going on shore by it, which, if the lights had not been there, would inevitably happened to their destruction.

This island, though seemingly miserable, and thinly inhabited, yet the inhabitants being almost all stone-cutters, we found there were no very poor people among them, and when they collected money for the re-building St. Paul's, they got more in this island than in the great town of Dorchester, as we were told.

Though Portland stands a league off from the mainland of Britain, yet it is almost joined by a prodigious riff of beach—that is to say, of small stones cast up by the sea—which runs from the island so near the shore of England that they ferry over with a boat and a rope, the water not being above half a stone's-throw over; and the said riff of beach ending, as it were, at that inlet of water, turns away west, and runs parallel with the shore quite to Abbotsbury, which is a town about seven miles beyond Weymouth.

I name this for two reasons: first, to explain again what I said before of ships being embayed and lost here. This is when ships coming from the westward omit to keep a good offing, or are taken short by contrary winds, and cannot weather the high land of Portland, but are driven between Portland and the mainland. If they can come to an anchor, and ride it out, well and good; and if not, they run on shore on that vast beach and are lost without remedy.

On the inside of this beach, and between it and the land, there is, as I have said, an inlet of water which they ferry over, as above, to pass and re-pass to and from Portland: this inlet opens at about two miles west, and grows very broad, and makes a kind of lake within the land of a mile and a half broad, and near three miles in length, the breadth unequal. At the farthest end west of this water is a large duck-coy, and the verge of the water well grown with wood, and proper groves of trees for cover for the fowl: in the open lake, or broad part, is a continual assembly of swans: here they live, feed, and breed, and the number of them is such that, I believe, I did not see so few as 7,000 or 8,000. Here they are protected, and here they breed in abundance. We saw several of them upon the wing, very high in the air, whence we supposed that they flew over the riff of beach, which parts the lake from the sea, to feed on the shores as they thought fit, and so came home again at their leisure.

From this duck-coy west, the lake narrows, and at last almost closes, till the beach joins the shore; and so Portland may be said, not to be an island, but part of the continent. And now we came to Abbotsbury, a town anciently famous for a great monastery, and now eminent for nothing but its ruins.

From hence we went on to Bridport, a pretty large corporation town on the sea-shore, though without a harbour. Here we saw boats all the way on the shore, fishing for mackerel, which they take in the easiest manner imaginable; for they fix one end of the net to a pole set deep into the sand, then, the net being in a boat, they row right out into the water some length, then turn and row parallel with the shore, veering out the net all the while, till they have let go all the net, except the line at the end, and then the boat rows on shore, when the men, hauling the net to the shore at both ends, bring to shore with it such fish as they surrounded in the little way they rowed. This, at that time, proved to be an incredible number, insomuch that the men could hardly draw them on shore. As soon as the boats had brought their fish on shore we observed a guard or watch placed on the shore in several places, who, we found, had their eye, not on the fishermen, but on the country people who came down to the shore to buy their fish; and very sharp we found they were, and some that came with small carts were obliged to go back empty without any fish. When we came to inquire into the particulars of this, we found that these were officers placed on the shore by the justices and magistrates of the towns about, who were ordered to prevent the country farmers buying the mackerel to dung their land with them, which was thought to be dangerous as to infection. In short, such was the plenty of fish that year that the mackerel, the finest and largest I ever saw, were sold at the seaside a hundred for a penny.

From Bridport (a town in which we see nothing remarkable) we came to Lyme, the town particularly made famous by the landing of the Duke of Monmouth and his unfortunate troops in the time of King James II., of which I need say nothing, the history of it being so recent in the memory of so many living.

This is a town of good figure, and has in it several eminent merchants who carry on a considerable trade to France, Spain, Newfoundland, and the Straits; and though they have neither creek or bay, road or river, they have a good harbour, but it is such a one as is not in all Britain besides, if there is such a one in any part of the world.

It is a massy pile of building, consisting of high and thick walls of stone, raised at first with all the methods that skill and art could devise, but maintained now with very little difficulty. The walls are raised in the main sea at a good distance from the shore; it consists of one main and solid wall of stone, large enough for carts and carriages to pass on the top, and to admit houses and warehouses to be built on it, so that it is broad as a street. Opposite to this, but farther into the sea, is another wall of the same workmanship, which crosses the end of the first wall and comes about with a tail parallel to the first wall.

Between the point of the first or main wall is the entrance into the port, and the second or opposite wall, breaking the violence of the sea from the entrance, the ships go into the basin as into a pier or harbour, and ride there as secure as in a millpond or as in a wet dock.

The townspeople have the benefit of this wonderful harbour, and it is carefully kept in repair, as indeed it behoves them to do; but they could give me nothing of the history of it, nor do they, as I could perceive, know anything of the original of it, or who built it. It was lately almost beaten down by a storm, but is repaired again.

This work is called the Cobb. The Custom House officers have a lodge and warehouse upon it, and there were several ships of very good force and rich in value in the basin of it when I was there. It might be strengthened with a fort, and the walls themselves are firm enough to carry what guns they please to plant upon it; but they did not seem to think it needful, and as the shore is convenient for batteries, they have some guns planted in proper places, both for the defence of the Cobb and the town also.

This town is under the government of a mayor and aldermen, and may pass for a place of wealth, considering the bigness of it. Here, we found, the merchants began to trade in the pilchard-fishing, though not to so considerable a degree as they do farther west—the pilchards seldom coming up so high eastward as Portland, and not very often so high as Lyme.

It was in sight of these hills that Queen Elizabeth's fleet, under the command of the Lord Howard of Effingham (then Admiral), began first to engage in a close and resolved fight with the invincible Spanish Armada in 1588, maintaining the fight, the Spaniards making eastward till they came the length of Portland Race, where they gave it over—the Spaniards having received considerable damage, and keeping then closer together. Off of the same place was a desperate engagement in the year 1672 between the English and Dutch, in which the Dutch were worsted and driven over to the coast of France, and then glad to make home to refit and repair.

While we stayed here some time viewing this town and coast, we had opportunity to observe the pleasant way of conversation as it is managed among the gentlemen of this county and their families, which are, without reflection, some of the most polite and well-bred people in the isle of Britain. As their hospitality is very great, and their bounty to the poor remarkable, so their generous friendly way of living with, visiting, and associating one with another is as hard to be described as it is really to be admired; they seem to have a mutual confidence in and friendship with one another, as if they were all relations; nor did I observe the sharping, tricking temper which is too much crept in among the gaming and horse-racing gentry in some parts of England to be so much known among them any otherwise than to be abhorred; and yet they sometimes play, too, and make matches and horse-races, as they see occasion.

The ladies here do not want the help of assemblies to assist in matchmaking, or half-pay officers to run away with their daughters, which the meetings called assemblies in some other parts of England are recommended for. Here is no Bury Fair, where the women are scandalously said to carry themselves to market, and where every night they meet at the play or at the assembly for intrigue; and yet I observed that the women do not seem to stick on hand so much in this country as in those countries where those assemblies are so lately set up—the reason of which, I cannot help saying, if my opinion may bear any weight, is that the Dorsetshire ladies are equal in beauty, and may be superior in reputation. In a word, their reputation seems here to be better kept, guarded by better conduct, and managed with more prudence; and yet the Dorsetshire ladies, I assure you, are not nuns; they do not go veiled about streets, or hide themselves when visited; but a general freedom of conversation—agreeable, mannerly, kind, and good—runs through the whole body of the gentry of both sexes, mixed with the best of behaviour, and yet governed by prudence and modesty such as I nowhere see better in all my observation through the whole isle of Britain. In this little interval also I visited some of the biggest towns in the north-west part of this county, as Blandford—a town on the River Stour in the road between Salisbury and Dorchester—a handsome well-built town, but chiefly famous for making the finest bone-lace in England, and where they showed me some so exquisitely fine as I think I never saw better in Flanders, France, or Italy, and which they said they rated at above £30 sterling a yard; but I suppose there was not much of this to be had. But it is most certain that they make exceeding rich lace in that county, such as no part of England can equal.

From thence I went west to Stourbridge, vulgarly called Strabridge. The town and the country around is employed in the manufacture of stockings, and which was once famous for making the finest, best, and highest-prize knit stocking in England; but that trade now is much decayed by the increase of the knitting-stocking engine or frame, which has destroyed the hand-knitting trade for fine stockings through the whole kingdom, of which I shall speak more in its place.

From hence I came to Sherborne, a large and populous town, with one collegiate or conventual church, and may properly claim to have more inhabitants in it than any town in Dorsetshire, though it is neither the county-town, nor does it send members to Parliament. The church is still a reverend pile, and shows the face of great antiquity. Here begins the Wiltshire medley clothing (though this town be in Dorsetshire), of which I shall speak at large in its place, and therefore I omit any discourse of it here.

Shaftesbury is also on the edge of this county, adjoining to Wiltshire and Dorsetshire, being fourteen miles from Salisbury, over that fine down or carpet ground which they call particularly or properly Salisbury Plain. It has neither house nor town in view all the way; and the road, which often lies very broad and branches off insensibly, might easily cause a traveller to lose his way. But there is a certain never-failing assistance upon all these downs for telling a stranger his way, and that is the number of shepherds feeding or keeping their vast flocks of sheep which are everywhere in the way, and who with a very little pains a traveller may always speak with. Nothing can be like it. The Arcadians' plains, of which we read so much pastoral trumpery in the poets, could be nothing to them.

This Shaftesbury is now a sorry town upon the top of a high hill, which closes the plain or downs, and whence Nature presents you a new scene or prospect—viz., of Somerset and Wiltshire—where it is all enclosed, and grown with woods, forests, and planted hedge-rows; the country rich, fertile, and populous; the towns and houses standing thick and being large and full of inhabitants, and those inhabitants fully employed in the richest and most valuable manufacture in the world—viz., the English clothing, as well the medley or mixed clothing as whites, as well for the home trade as the foreign trade, of which I shall take leave to be very particular in my return through the west and north part of Wiltshire in the latter part of this work.

In my return to my western progress, I passed some little part of Somersetshire, as through Evil or Yeovil, upon the River Ivil, in going to which we go down a long steep hill, which they call Babylon Hill, but from what original I could find none of the country people to inform me.

This Yeovil is a market-town of good resort; and some clothing is carried on in and near it, but not much. Its main manufacture at this time is making of gloves.

It cannot pass my observation here that when we are come this length from London the dialect of the English tongue, or the country way of expressing themselves, is not easily understood—it is so strangely altered. It is true that it is so in many parts of England besides, but in none in so gross a degree as in this part. This way of boorish country speech, as in Ireland it is called the "brogue" upon the tongue, so here it is called "jouring;" and it is certain that though the tongue be all mere natural English, yet those that are but a little acquainted with them cannot understand one-half of what they say. It is not possible to explain this fully by writing, because the difference is not so much in the orthography of words as in the tone and diction—their abridging the speech, "cham" for "I am," "chil" for "I will," "don" for "put on," and "doff" for "put off," and the like. And I cannot omit a short story here on this subject. Coming to a relation's house, who was a school-master at Martock, in Somersetshire, I went into his school to beg the boys a play-day, as is usual in such cases (I should have said, to beg the master a play-day. But that by the way). Coming into the school, I observed one of the lowest scholars was reading his lesson to the usher, which lesson, it seems, was a chapter in the Bible. So I sat down by the master till the boy had read out his chapter. I observed the boy read a little oddly in the tone of the country, which made me the more attentive, because on inquiry I found that the words were the same and the orthography the same as in all our Bibles. I observed also the boy read it out with his eyes still on the book and his head (like a mere boy) moving from side to side as the lines reached cross the columns of the book. His lesson was in the Canticles, v. 3 of chap. v. The words these:—"I have put off my coat. How shall I put it on? I have washed my feet. How shall I defile them?"

The boy read thus, with his eyes, as I say, full on the text:—"Chav a doffed my cooat. How shall I don't? Chav a washed my veet. How shall I moil 'em?"

How the dexterous dunce could form his month to express so readily the words (which stood right printed in the book) in his country jargon, I could not but admire. I shall add to this another piece as diverting, which also happened in my knowledge at this very town of Yeovil, though some years ago.

There lived a good substantial family in the town not far from the "Angel Inn"—a well-known house, which was then, and, I suppose, is still, the chief inn of the town. This family had a dog which, among his other good qualities for which they kept him (for he was a rare house-dog), had this bad one—that he was a most notorious thief, but withal so cunning a dog, and managed himself so warily, that he preserved a mighty good reputation among the neighbourhood. As the family was well beloved in the town, so was the dog. He was known to be a very useful servant to them, especially in the night (when he was fierce as a lion; but in the day the gentlest, lovingest creature that could be), and, as they said, all the neighbours had a good word for this dog.

It happened that the good wife or mistress at the "Angel Inn" had frequently missed several pieces of meat out of the pail, as they say—or powdering-tub, as we call it—and that some were very large pieces. It is also to be observed the dog did not stay to eat what he took upon the spot, in which case some pieces or bones or fragments might be left, and so it might be discovered to be a dog; but he made cleaner work, and when he fastened upon a piece of meat he was sure to carry it quite away to such retreats as he knew he could be safe in, and so feast upon it at leisure.

It happened at last, as with most thieves it does, that the inn-keeper was too cunning for him, and the poor dog was nabbed, taken in the fact, and could make no defence.

Having found the thief and got him in custody, the master of the house, a good-humoured fellow, and loth to disoblige the dog's master by executing the criminal, as the dog law directs, mitigates his sentence, and handled him as follows:—First, taking out his knife, he cut off both his ears; and then, bringing him to the threshold, he chopped off his tail. And having thus effectually dishonoured the poor cur among his neighbours, he tied a string about his neck, and a piece of paper to the string, directed to his master, and with these witty West Country verses on it:—

"To my honoured master, --- Esq.
"Hail master a cham a' com hoam,
So cut as an ape, and tail have I noan,
For stealing of beef and pork out of the pail,
For thease they'v cut my ears, for th' wother my tail;
Nea measter, and us tell thee more nor that
And's come there again, my brains will be flat."

I could give many more accounts of the different dialects of the people of this country, in some of which they are really not to be understood; but the particulars have little or no diversion in them. They carry it such a length that we see their "jouring" speech even upon their monuments and gravestones; as, for example, even in some of the churchyards of the city of Bristol I saw this excellent poetry after some other lines:—

"And when that thou doest hear of thick,
Think of the glass that runneth quick."

But I proceed into Devonshire. From Yeovil we came to Crookorn, thence to Chard, and from thence into the same road I was in before at Honiton.

This is a large and beautiful market-town, very populous and well built, and is so very remarkably paved with small pebbles that on either side the way a little channel is left shouldered up on the sides of it, so that it holds a small stream of fine clear running water, with a little square dipping-place left at every door; so that every family in the town has a clear, clean running river (as it may be called) just at their own door, and this so much finer, so much pleasanter, and agreeable to look on than that at Salisbury (which they boast so much of), that, in my opinion, there is no comparison.

Here we see the first of the great serge manufacture of Devonshire—a trade too great to be described in miniature, as it must be if I undertake it here, and which takes up this whole county, which is the largest and most populous in England, Yorkshire excepted (which ought to be esteemed three counties, and is, indeed, divided as such into the East, West, and North Riding). But Devonshire, one entire county, is so full of great towns, and those towns so full of people, and those people so universally employed in trade and manufactures, that not only it cannot be equalled in England, but perhaps not in Europe.

In my travel through Dorsetshire I ought to have observed that the biggest towns in that county sent no members to Parliament, and that the smallest did—that is to say that Sherborne, Blandford, Wimborneminster, Stourminster, and several other towns choose no members; whereas Weymouth, Melcombe, and Bridport were all burgess towns. But now we come to Devonshire we find almost all the great towns, and some smaller, choosing members also. It is true there are some large populous towns that do not choose, but then there are so many that do, that the county seems to have no injustice, for they send up six-and-twenty members.

However, as I say above, there are several great towns which do not choose Parliament men, of which Bideford is one, Crediton or Kirton another, Ilfracombe a third; but, those excepted, the principal towns in the county do all choose members of Parliament.

Honiton is one of those, and may pass not only for a pleasant good town, as before, but stands in the best and pleasantest part of the whole county, and I cannot but recommend it to any gentlemen that travel this road, that if they please to observe the prospect for half a mile till their coming down the hill and to the entrance into Honiton, the view of the country is the most beautiful landscape in the world—a mere picture—and I do not remember the like in any one place in England. It is observable that the market of this town was kept originally on the Sunday, till it was changed by the direction of King John.

From Honiton the country is exceeding pleasant still, and on the road they have a beautiful prospect almost all the way to Exeter (which is twelve miles). On the left-hand of this road lies that part of the county which they call the South Hams, and which is famous for the best cider in that part of England; also the town of St.-Mary-Ottery, commonly called St. Mary Autree. They tell us the name is derived from the River Ottery, and that from the multitude of otters found always in that river, which however, to me, seems fabulous. Nor does there appear to be any such great number of otters in that water, or in the county about, more than is usual in other counties or in other parts of the county about them. They tell us they send twenty thousand hogsheads of cider hence every year to London, and (which is still worse) that it is most of it bought there by the merchants to mix with their wines—which, if true, is not much to the reputation of the London vintners. But that by-the-bye.

From hence we came to Exeter, a city famous for two things which we seldom find unite in the same town—viz., that it is full of gentry and good company, and yet full of trade and manufactures also. The serge market held here every week is very well worth a stranger's seeing, and next to the Brigg Market at Leeds, in Yorkshire, is the greatest in England. The people assured me that at this market is generally sold from sixty to seventy to eighty, and sometimes a hundred, thousand pounds value in serges in a week. I think it is kept on Mondays.

They have the River Esk here, a very considerable river, and principal in the whole county; and within three miles, or thereabouts, it receives ships of any ordinary burthen, the port there being called Topsham. But now by the application, and at the expense, of the citizens the channel of the river is so widened, deepened, and cleansed from the shoal, which would otherwise interrupt the navigation, that the ships come now quite up to the city, and there with ease both deliver and take in their lading.

This city drives a very great correspondence with Holland, as also directly to Portugal, Spain, and Italy—shipping off vast quantities of their woollen manufactures especially to Holland, the Dutch giving very large commissions here for the buying of serges perpetuans, and such goods; which are made not only in and about Exeter, but at Crediton, Honiton, Culliton, St.-Mary-Ottery, Newton Bushel, Ashburton, and especially at Tiverton, Cullompton, Bampton, and all the north-east part of the county—which part of the county is, as it may be said, fully employed, the people made rich, and the poor that are properly so called well subsisted and employed by it.

Exeter is a large, rich, beautiful, populous, and was once a very strong city; but as to the last, as the castle, the walls, and all the old works are demolished, so, were they standing, the way of managing sieges and attacks of towns is such now, and so altered from what it was in those days, that Exeter in the utmost strength it could ever boast would not now hold out five days open trenches—nay, would hardly put an army to the trouble of opening trenches against it at all. This city was famous in the late civil unnatural war for its loyalty to the king, and for being a sanctuary to the queen, where her Majesty resided for some time, and here she was delivered of a daughter, being the Princess Henrietta Maria, of whom our histories give a particular account, so I need say no more of it here.

The cathedral church of this city is an ancient beauty, or, as it may be said, it is beautiful for its antiquity; but it has been so fully and often described that it would look like a mere copying from others to mention it. There is a good library kept in it, in which are some manuscripts, and particularly an old missal or mass-book, the leaves of vellum, and famous for its most exquisite writing.

This county, and this part of it in particular, has been famous for the birth of several eminent men as well for learning as for arts and for war, as particularly:—

1. Sir William Petre, who the learned Dr. Wake (now Archbishop of Canterbury, and author of the Additions to Mr. Camden) says was Secretary of State and Privy Councillor to King Henry VIII., Edward VI., Queen Mary, and Queen Elizabeth, and seven times sent ambassador into foreign countries.

2. Sir Thomas Bodley, famous and of grateful memory to all learned men and lovers of letters for his collecting and establishing the best library in Britain, which is now at Oxford, and is called, after his name, the Bodleian Library to this day.

3. Also Sir Francis Drake, born at Plymouth.

4. Sir Walter Raleigh. Of both those I need say nothing; fame publishes their merit upon every mention of their names.

5. That great patron of learning, Richard Hooker, author of the "Ecclesiastical Polity," and of several other valuable pieces.

6. Of Dr. Arthur Duck, a famed civilian, and well known by his works among the learned advocates of Doctors' Commons.

7. Dr. John Moreman, of Southold, famous for being the first clergyman in England who ventured to teach his parishioners the Lord's Prayer, Creed, and Ten Commandments in the English tongue, and reading them so publicly in the parish church of Mayenhennet in this county, of which he was vicar.

8. Dr. John de Brampton, a man of great learning who flourished in the reign of Henry VI., was famous for being the first that read Aristotle publicly in the University of Cambridge, and for several learned books of his writing, which are now lost.

9. Peter Blundel, a clothier, who built the free school at Tiverton, and endowed it very handsomely; of which in its place.

10. Sir John Glanvill, a noted lawyer, and one of the Judges of the Common Pleas.

11. Sergeant Glanvill, his son; as great a lawyer as his father.

12. Sir John Maynard, an eminent lawyer of later years; one of the Commissioners of the Great Seal under King William III. All these three were born at Tavistock.

13. Sir Peter King, the present Lord Chief Justice of the Common Pleas. And many others.

I shall take the north part of this county in my return from Cornwall; so I must now lean to the south—that is to say, to the South Coast—for in going on indeed we go south-west.

About twenty-two miles from Exeter we go to Totnes, on the River Dart. This is a very good town, of some trade; but has more gentlemen in it than tradesmen of note. They have a very fine stone bridge here over the river, which, being within seven or eight miles of the sea, is very large; and the tide flows ten or twelve feet at the bridge. Here we had the diversion of seeing them catch fish with the assistance of a dog. The case is this:—On the south side of the river, and on a slip, or narrow cut or channel made on purpose for a mill, there stands a corn-mill; the mill-tail, or floor for the water below the wheels, is wharfed up on either side with stone above high-water mark, and for above twenty or thirty feet in length below it on that part of the river towards the sea; at the end of this wharfing is a grating of wood, the cross-bars of which stand bearing inward, sharp at the end, and pointing inward towards one another, as the wires of a mouse-trap.

When the tide flows up, the fish can with ease go in between the points of these cross-bars, but the mill being shut down they can go no farther upwards; and when the water ebbs again, they are left behind, not being able to pass the points of the grating, as above, outwards; which, like a mouse-trap, keeps them in, so that they are left at the bottom with about a foot or a foot and a half of water. We were carried hither at low water, where we saw about fifty or sixty small salmon, about seventeen to twenty inches long, which the country people call salmon-peal; and to catch these the person who went with us, who was our landlord at a great inn next the bridge, put in a net on a hoop at the end of a pole, the pole going cross the hoop (which we call in this country a shove-net). The net being fixed at one end of the place, they put in a dog (who was taught his trade beforehand) at the other end of the place, and he drives all the fish into the net; so that, only holding the net still in its place, the man took up two or three and thirty salmon-peal at the first time.

Of these we took six for our dinner, for which they asked a shilling (viz., twopence a-piece); and for such fish, not at all bigger, and not so fresh, I have seen six-and-sixpence each given at a London fish-market, whither they are sometimes brought from Chichester by land carriage.

This excessive plenty of so good fish (and other provisions being likewise very cheap in proportion) makes the town of Totnes a very good place to live in; especially for such as have large families and but small estates. And many such are said to come into those parts on purpose for saving money, and to live in proportion to their income.

From hence we went still south about seven miles (all in view of this river) to Dartmouth, a town of note, seated at the mouth of the River Dart, and where it enters into the sea at a very narrow but safe entrance. The opening into Dartmouth Harbour is not broad, but the channel deep enough for the biggest ship in the Royal Navy. The sides of the entrance are high-mounded with rocks, without which, just at the first narrowing of the passage, stands a good strong fort without a platform of guns, which commands the port.

The narrow entrance is not much above half a mile, when it opens and makes a basin or harbour able to receive 500 sail of ships of any size, and where they may ride with the greatest safety, even as in a mill-pond or wet dock. I had the curiosity here, with the assistance of a merchant of the town, to go out to the mouth of the haven in a boat to see the entrance, and castle or fort that commands it; and coming back with the tide of flood, I observed some small fish to skip and play upon the surface of the water, upon which I asked my friend what fish they were. Immediately one of the rowers or seamen starts up in the boat, and, throwing his arms abroad as if he had been bewitched, cries out as loud as he could bawl, "A school! a school!" The word was taken to the shore as hastily as it would have been on land if he had cried "Fire!" And by that time we reached the quays the town was all in a kind of an uproar.

The matter was that a great shoal—or, as they call it, a "school"—of pilchards came swimming with the tide of flood, directly out of the sea into the harbour. My friend whose boat we were in told me this was a surprise which he would have been very glad of if he could but have had a day or two's warning, for he might have taken 200 tons of them. And the like was the case of other merchants in town; for, in short, nobody was ready for them, except a small fishing-boat or two—one of which went out into the middle of the harbour, and at two or three hauls took about forty thousand of them. We sent our servant to the quay to buy some, who for a halfpenny brought us seventeen, and, if he would have taken them, might have had as many more for the same money. With these we went to dinner; the cook at the inn broiled them for us, which is their way of dressing them, with pepper and salt, which cost us about a farthing; so that two of us and a servant dined— and at a tavern, too—for three farthings, dressing and all. And this is the reason of telling the tale. What drink—wine or beer—we had I do not remember; but, whatever it was, that we paid for by itself. But for our food we really dined for three farthings, and very well, too. Our friend treated us the next day with a dish of large lobsters, and I being curious to know the value of such things, and having freedom enough with him to inquire, I found that for 6d. or 8d. they bought as good lobsters there as would have cost in London 3s. to 3s. 6d. each.

In observing the coming in of those pilchards, as above, we found that out at sea, in the offing, beyond the mouth of the harbour, there was a whole army of porpoises, which, as they told us, pursued the pilchards, and, it is probable, drove them into the harbour, as above. The school, it seems, drove up the river a great way, even as high as Totnes Bridge, as we heard afterwards; so that the country people who had boats and nets catched as many as they knew what to do with, and perhaps lived upon pilchards for several days. But as to the merchants and trade, their coming was so sudden that it was no advantage to them.

Round the west side of this basin or harbour, in a kind of a semicircle, lies the town of Dartmouth, a very large and populous town, though but meanly built, and standing on the side of a steep hill; yet the quay is large, and the street before it spacious. Here are some very flourishing merchants, who trade very prosperously, and to the most considerable trading ports of Spain, Portugal, Italy, and the Plantations; but especially they are great traders to Newfoundland, and from thence to Spain and Italy, with fish; and they drive a good trade also in their own fishery of pilchards, which is hereabouts carried on with the greatest number of vessels of any port in the west, except Falmouth.

A little to the southward of this town, and to the east of the port, is Tor Bay, of which I know nothing proper to my observation, more than that it is a very good road for ships, though sometimes (especially with a southerly or south-east wind) ships have been obliged to quit the bay and put out to sea, or run into Dartmouth for shelter.

I suppose I need not mention that they had from the hilly part of this town, and especially from the hills opposite to it, the noble prospect, and at that time particularly delightful, of the Prince of Orange's fleet when he came to that coast, and as they entered into Tor Bay to land—the Prince and his army being in a fleet of about 600 sail of transport ships, besides 50 sail of men-of-war of the line, all which, with a fair wind and fine weather, came to an anchor there at once.

This town, as most of the towns of Devonshire are, is full of Dissenters, and a very large meeting-house they have here. How they act here with respect to the great dispute about the doctrine of the Trinity, which has caused such a breach among those people at Exeter and other parts of the county, I cannot give any account of. This town sends two members to Parliament.

From hence we went to Plympton, a poor and thinly-inhabited town, though blessed with the like privilege of sending members to the Parliament, of which I have little more to say but that from thence the road lies to Plymouth, distance about six miles.

Plymouth is indeed a town of consideration, and of great importance to the public. The situation of it between two very large inlets of the sea, and in the bottom of a large bay, which is very remarkable for the advantage of navigation. The Sound or Bay is compassed on every side with hills, and the shore generally steep and rocky, though the anchorage is good, and it is pretty safe riding. In the entrance to this bay lies a large and most dangerous rock, which at high-water is covered, but at low-tide lies bare, where many a good ship has been lost, even in the view of safety, and many a ship's crew drowned in the night, before help could be had for them.

Upon this rock (which was called the Eddystone, from its situation) the famous Mr. Winstanley undertook to build a lighthouse for the direction of sailors, and with great art and expedition finished it; which work—considering its height, the magnitude of its building, and the little hold there was by which it was possible to fasten it to the rock—stood to admiration, and bore out many a bitter storm.

Mr. Winstanley often visited, and frequently strengthened, the building by new works, and was so confident of its firmness and stability that he usually said he only desired to be in it when a storm should happen; for many people had told him it would certainly fall if it came to blow a little harder than ordinary.

But he happened at last to be in it once too often—namely, when that dreadful tempest blew, November 27, 1703. This tempest began on the Wednesday before, and blew with such violence, and shook the lighthouse so much, that, as they told me there, Mr. Winstanley would fain have been on shore, and made signals for help; but no boats durst go off to him; and, to finish the tragedy, on the Friday, November 26, when the tempest was so redoubled that it became a terror to the whole nation, the first sight there seaward that the people of Plymouth were presented with in the morning after the storm was the bare Eddystone, the lighthouse being gone; in which Mr. Winstanley and all that were with him perished, and were never seen or heard of since. But that which was a worse loss still was that, a few days after, a merchant's ship called the Winchelsea, homeward bound from Virginia, not knowing the Eddystone lighthouse was down, for want of the light that should have been seen, run foul of the rock itself, and was lost with all her lading and most of her men. But there is now another light-house built on the same rock.

What other disasters happened at the same time in the Sound and in the roads about Plymouth is not my business; they are also published in other books, to which I refer.

One thing which I was a witness to on a former journey to this place, I cannot omit. It was the next year after that great storm, and but a little sooner in the year, being in August; I was at Plymouth, and walking on the Hoo (which is a plain on the edge of the sea, looking to the road), I observed the evening so serene, so calm, so bright, and the sea so smooth, that a finer sight, I think, I never saw. There was very little wind, but what was, seemed to be westerly; and about an hour after, it blew a little breeze at south-west, with which wind there came into the Sound that night and the next morning a fleet of fourteen sail of ships from Barbadoes, richly laden for London. Having been long at sea, most of the captains and passengers came on shore to refresh themselves, as is usual after such tedious voyages; and the ships rode all in the Sound on that side next to Catwater. As is customary upon safe arriving to their native country, there was a general joy and rejoicing both on board and on shore.

The next day the wind began to freshen, especially in the afternoon, and the sea to be disturbed, and very hard it blew at night; but all was well for that time. But the night after, it blew a dreadful storm (not much inferior, for the time it lasted, to the storm mentioned above which blew down the lighthouse on the Eddystone). About mid-night the noise, indeed, was very dreadful, what with the rearing of the sea and of the wind, intermixed with the firing of guns for help from the ships, the cries of the seamen and people on shore, and (which was worse) the cries of those which were driven on shore by the tempest and dashed in pieces. In a word, all the fleet except three, or thereabouts, were dashed to pieces against the rocks and sunk in the sea, most of the men being drowned. Those three who were saved, received so much damage that their lading was almost all spoiled. One ship in the dark of the night, the men not knowing where they were, run into Catwater, and run on shore there; by which she was, however, saved from shipwreck, and the lives of her crew were saved also.

This was a melancholy morning indeed. Nothing was to be seen but wrecks of the ships and a foaming, furious sea in that very place where they rode all in joy and triumph but the evening before. The captains, passengers, and officers who were, as I have said, gone on shore, between the joy of saving their lives, and the affliction of having lost their ships, their cargoes, and their friends, were objects indeed worth our compassion and observation. And there was a great variety of the passions to be observed in them—now lamenting their losses, their giving thanks for their deliverance. Many of the passengers had lost their all, and were, as they expressed themselves, "utterly undone." They were, I say, now lamenting their losses with violent excesses of grief; then giving thanks for their lives, and that they should be brought on shore, as it were, on purpose to be saved from death; then again in tears for such as were drowned. The various cases were indeed very affecting, and, in many things, very instructing.

As I say, Plymouth lies in the bottom of this Sound, in the centre between the two waters, so there lies against it, in the same position, an island, which they call St. Nicholas, on which there is a castle which commands the entrance into Hamoaze, and indeed that also into Catwater in some degree. In this island the famous General Lambert, one of Cromwell's great agents or officers in the rebellion, was imprisoned for life, and lived many years there.

On the shore over against this island is the citadel of Plymouth, a small but regular fortification, inaccessible by sea, but not exceeding strong by land, except that they say the works are of a stone hard as marble, and would not seen yield to the batteries of an enemy—but that is a language our modern engineers now laugh at.

The town stands above this, upon the same rock, and lies sloping on the side of it, towards the east—the inlet of the sea which is called Catwater, and which is a harbour capable of receiving any number of ships and of any size, washing the eastern shore of the town, where they have a kind of natural mole or haven, with a quay and all other conveniences for bringing in vessels for loading and unloading; nor is the trade carried on here inconsiderable in itself, or the number of merchants small.

The other inlet of the sea, as I term it, is on the other side of the town, and is called Hamoaze, being the mouth of the River Tamar, a considerable river which parts the two counties of Devon and Cornwall. Here (the war with France making it necessary that the ships of war should have a retreat nearer hand than at Portsmouth) the late King William ordered a wet dock—with yards, dry docks, launches, and conveniences of all kinds for building and repairing of ships—to be built; and with these followed necessarily the building of store-houses and warehouses for the rigging, sails, naval and military stores, &c., of such ships as may be appointed to be laid up there, as now several are; with very handsome houses for the commissioners, clerks, and officers of all kinds usual in the king's yards, to dwell in. It is, in short, now become as complete an arsenal or yard for building and fitting men-of-war as any the Government are masters of, and perhaps much more convenient than some of them, though not so large.

The building of these things, with the addition of rope-walks and mast-yards, &c., as it brought abundance of trades-people and workmen to the place, so they began by little and little to build houses on the lands adjacent, till at length there appeared a very handsome street, spacious and large, and as well inhabited; and so many houses are since added that it is become a considerable town, and must of consequence in time draw abundance of people from Plymouth itself.

However, the town of Plymouth is, and will always be, a very considerable town, while that excellent harbour makes it such a general port for the receiving all the fleets of merchants' ships from the southward (as from Spain, Italy, the West Indies, &c.), who generally make it the first port to put in at for refreshment, or safety from either weather or enemies.

The town is populous and wealthy, having, as above, several considerable merchants and abundance of wealthy shopkeepers, whose trade depends upon supplying the sea-faring people that upon so many occasions put into that port. As for gentlemen—I mean, those that are such by family and birth and way of living—it cannot be expected to find many such in a town merely depending on trade, shipping, and sea-faring business; yet I found here some men of value (persons of liberal education, general knowledge, and excellent behaviour), whose society obliges me to say that a gentleman might find very agreeable company in Plymouth.

From Plymouth we pass the Tamar over a ferry to Saltash—a little, poor, shattered town, the first we set foot on in the county of Cornwall. The Tamar here is very wide, and the ferry-boats bad; so that I thought myself well escaped when I got safe on shore in Cornwall.

Saltash seems to be the ruins of a larger place; and we saw many houses, as it were, falling down, and I doubt not but the mice and rats have abandoned many more, as they say they will when they are likely to fall. Yet this town is governed by a mayor and aldermen, has many privileges, sends members to Parliament, takes toll of all vessels that pass the river, and have the sole oyster-fishing in the whole river, which is considerable. Mr. Carew, author of the "Survey of Cornwall," tells us a strange story of a dog in this town, of whom it was observed that if they gave him any large bone or piece of meat, he immediately went out of doors with it, and after having disappeared for some time would return again; upon which, after some time, they watched him, when, to their great surprise, they found that the poor charitable creature carried what he so got to an old decrepit mastiff, which lay in a nest that he had made among the brakes a little way out of the town, and was blind, so that he could not help himself; and there this creature fed him. He adds also that on Sundays or holidays, when he found they made good cheer in the house where he lived, he would go out and bring this old blind dog to the door, and feed him there till he had enough, and then go with him back to his habitation in the country again, and see him safe in. If this story is true, it is very remarkable indeed; and I thought it worth telling, because the author was a person who, they say, might be credited.

**69**

This town has a kind of jurisdiction upon the River Tamar down to the mouth of the port, so that they claim anchorage of all small ships that enter the river; their coroner sits upon all dead bodies that are found drowned in the river and the like, but they make not much profit of them. There is a good market here, and that is the best thing to be said of the town; it is also very much increased since the number of the inhabitants are increased at the new town, as I mentioned as near the dock at the mouth of Hamoaze, for those people choose rather to go to Saltash to market by water than to walk to Plymouth by land for their provisions. Because, first, as they go in the town boat, the same boat brings home what they buy, so that it is much less trouble; second, because provisions are bought much cheaper at Saltash than at Plymouth. This, I say, is like to be a very great advantage to the town of Saltash, and may in time put a new face of wealth upon the place.

They talk of some merchants beginning to trade here, and they have some ships that use the Newfoundland fishery; but I could not hear of anything considerable they do in it. There is no other considerable town up the Tamar till we come to Launceston, the county town, which I shall take in my return; so I turned west, keeping the south shore of the county to the Land's End.

From Saltash I went to Liskeard, about seven miles. This is a considerable town, well built; has people of fashion in it, and a very great market; it also sends two members to Parliament, and is one of the five towns called Stannary Towns—that is to say, where the blocks of tin are brought to the coinage; of which, by itself, this coinage of tin is an article very much to the advantage of the towns where it is settled, though the money paid goes another way.

This town of Liskeard was once eminent, had a good castle, and a large house, where the ancient Dukes of Cornwall kept their court in those days; also it enjoyed several privileges, especially by the favour of the Black Prince, who as Prince of Wales and Duke of Cornwall resided here. And in return they say this town and the country round it raised a great body of stout young fellows, who entered into his service and followed his fortunes in his wars in France, as also in Spain. But these buildings are so decayed that there are now scarce any of the ruins of the castle or of the prince's court remaining.

The only public edifices they have now to show are the guild or town hall, on which there is a turret with a fine clock; a very good free school, well provided; a very fine conduit in the market-place; an ancient large church; and, which is something rare for the county of Cornwall, a large, new-built meeting-house for the Dissenters, which I name because they assured me there was but three more, and those very inconsiderable, in all the county of Cornwall; whereas in Devonshire, which is the next county, there are reckoned about seventy, some of which are exceeding large and fine.

This town is also remarkable for a very great trade in all manufactures of leather, such as boots, shoes, gloves, purses, breaches, &c.; and some spinning of late years is set up here, encouraged by the woollen manufacturers of Devonshire.

Between these two towns of Saltash and Liskeard is St. Germans, now a village, decayed, and without any market, but the largest parish in the whole county—in the bounds of which is contained, as they report, seventeen villages, and the town of Saltash among them; for Saltash has no parish church, it seems, of itself, but as a chapel-of-ease to St. Germans. In the neighbourhood of these towns are many pleasant seats of the Cornish gentry, who are indeed very numerous, though their estates may not be so large as is usual in England; yet neither are they despicable in that part; and in particular this may be said of them—that as they generally live cheap, and are more at home than in other counties, so they live more like gentlemen, and keep more within bounds of their estates than the English generally do, take them all together.

Add to this that they are the most sociable, generous, and to one another the kindest, neighbours that are to be found; and as they generally live, as we may say, together (for they are almost always at one another's houses), so they generally intermarry among themselves, the gentlemen seldom going out of the county for a wife, or the ladies for a husband; from whence they say that proverb upon them was raised, viz., "That all the Cornish gentlemen are cousins."

On the hills north of Liskeard, and in the way between Liskeard and Launceston, there are many tin-mines. And, as they told us, some of the richest veins of that metal are found there that are in the whole county—the metal, when cast at the blowing houses into blocks, being, as above, carried to Liskeard to be coined.

From Liskeard, in our course west, we are necessarily carried to the sea-coast, because of the River Fowey or Fowath, which empties itself into the sea at a very large mouth. And hereby this river rising in the middle of the breadth of the county and running south, and the River Camel rising not far from it and running north, with a like large channel, the land from Bodmin to the western part of the county is almost made an island and in a manner cut off from the eastern part—the peninsula, or neck of land between, being not above twelve miles over.

On this south side we came to Foy or Fowey, an ancient town, and formerly very large—nay, not large only, but powerful and potent; for the Foyens, as they were then called, were able to fit out large fleets, not only for merchants' ships, but even of men-of-war; and with these not only fought with, but several times vanquished and routed, the squadron of the Cinque Ports men, who in those days were thought very powerful.

Mr. Camden observes that the town of Foy quarters some part of the arms of every one of those Cinque Ports with their own, intimating that they had at several times trampled over them all. Certain it is they did often beat them, and took their ships, and brought them as good prizes into their haven of Foy; and carried it so high that they fitted out their fleets against the French, and took several of their men-of-war when they were at war with England, and enriched their town by the spoil of their enemies.

Edward IV. favoured them much; and because the French threatened them to come up their river with a powerful navy to burn their town, he caused two forts to be built at the public charge for security of the town and river, which forts—at least, some show of them—remain there still. But the same King Edward was some time after so disgusted at the townsmen for officiously falling upon the French, after a truce was made and proclaimed, that he effectually disarmed them, took away their whole fleet, ships, tackle, apparel, and furniture; and since that time we do not read of any of their naval exploits, nor that they ever recovered or attempted to recover their strength at sea. However, Foy at this time is a very fair town; it lies extended on the east side of the river for above a mile, the buildings fair. And there are a great many flourishing merchants in it, who have a great share in the fishing trade, especially for pilchards, of which they take a great quantity hereabouts. In this town is also a coinage for the tin, of which a great quantity is dug up in the country north and west of the town.

The River Fowey, which is very broad and deep here, was formerly navigable by ships of good burthen as high as Lostwithiel—an ancient and once a flourishing but now a decayed town; and as to trade and navigation, quite destitute; which is occasioned by the river being filled up with sands, which, some say, the tides drive up in stormy weather from the sea; others say it is by sands washed from the lead-mines in the hills; the last of which, by the way, I take to be a mistake, the sand from the hills being not of quantity sufficient to fill up the channel of a navigable river, and, if it had, might easily have been stopped by the townspeople from falling into the river. But that the sea has choked up the river with sand is not only probable, but true; and there are other rivers which suffer in the like manner in this same country.

This town of Lostwithiel retains, however, several advantages which support its figure—as, first, that it is one of the Coinage Towns, as I call them; or Stannary Towns, as others call them; (2) the common gaol for the whole Stannary is here, as are also the County Courts for the whole county of Cornwall.

There is a mock cavalcade kept up at this town, which is very remarkable. The particulars, as they are related by Mr. Carew in his "Survey of Cornwall," take as follows:—

"Upon Little Easter Sunday the freeholders of this town and manor, by themselves or their deputies, did there assemble; amongst whom one (as it fell to his lot by turn), bravely apparelled, gallantly mounted, with a crown on his head, a sceptre in his hand, and a sword borne before him, and dutifully attended by all the rest (also on horseback), rode through the principal street to the church. The curate in his best beseen solemnly received him at the churchyard stile, and conducted him to hear divine service. After which he repaired, with the same pomp, to a house provided for that purpose, made a feast to his attendants, kept the table's-end himself, and was served with kneeling assay and all other rights due to the estate of a prince; with which dinner the ceremony ended, and every man returned home again. The pedigree of this usage is derived from so many descents of ages that the cause and author outreach the remembrance. Howbeit, these circumstances afford a conjecture that it should betoken royalties appertaining to the honour of Cornwall."

Behind Foy and nearer to the coast, at the mouth of a small river which some call Lowe, though without any authority, there stand two towns opposite to one another bearing the name of the River Looe—that is to say, distinguished by the addition of East Looe and West Looe. These are both good trading towns, and especially fishing towns; and, which is very particular, are (like Weymouth and Melcombe, in Dorsetshire) separated only by the creek or river, and yet each of them sends members to Parliament. These towns are joined together by a very beautiful and stately stone bridge having fifteen arches.

East Looe was the ancienter corporation of the two, and for some ages ago the greater and more considerable town; but now they tell us West Looe is the richest, and has the most ships belonging to it. Were they put together, they would make a very handsome seaport town. They have a great fishing trade here, as well for supply of the country as for merchandise, and the towns are not despisable. But as to sending four members to the British Parliament (which is as many as the City of London chooses), that, I confess, seems a little scandalous; but to whom, is none of my business to inquire.

Passing from hence, and ferrying over Foy River or the River Foweth (call it as you please), we come into a large country without many towns in it of note, but very well furnished with gentlemen's seats, and a little higher up with tin-works.

The sea making several deep bays here, they who travel by land are obliged to go higher into the country to pass above the water, especially at Trewardreth Bay, which lies very broad, above ten miles within the country, which passing at Trewardreth (a town of no great note, though the bay takes its name from it), the next inlet of the sea is the famous firth or inlet called Falmouth Haven. It is certainly, next to Milford Haven in South Wales, the fairest and best road for shipping that is in the whole isle of Britain, whether be considered the depth of water for above twenty miles within land; the safety of riding, sheltered from all kind of winds or storms; the good anchorage; and the many creeks, all navigable, where ships may run in and be safe; so that the like is nowhere to be found.

There are six or seven very considerable places upon this haven and the rivers from it—viz., Grampound, Tregony, Truro, Penryn, Falmouth, St. Maws, and Pendennis. The three first of these send members to Parliament. The town of Falmouth, as big as all the three, and richer than ten of them, sends none; which imports no more than this—that Falmouth itself is not of so great antiquity as to its rising as those other towns are; and yet the whole haven takes its name from Falmouth, too, unless, as some think, the town took its name from the haven, which, however, they give no authority to suggest.

St. Maws and Pendennis are two fortifications placed at the points or entrance of this haven, opposite to one another, though not with a communication or view; they are very strong—the first principally by sea, having a good platform of guns pointing athwart the Channel, and planted on a level with the water. But Pendennis Castle is strong by land as well as by water, is regularly fortified, has good out-works, and generally a strong garrison. St. Maws, otherwise called St. Mary's, has a town annexed to the castle, and is a borough sending members to the Parliament. Pendennis is a mere fortress, though there are some habitations in it, too, and some at a small distance near the seaside, but not of any great consideration.

The town of Falmouth is by much the richest and best trading town in this county, though not so ancient as its neighbour town of Truro; and indeed is in some things obliged to acknowledge the seigniority—namely, that in the corporation of Truro the person whom they choose to be their Mayor of Truro is also Mayor of Falmouth of course. How the jurisdiction is managed is an account too long for this place. The Truro-men also receive several duties collected in Falmouth, particularly wharfage for the merchandises landed or shipped off; but let these advantages be what they will, the town of Falmouth has gotten the trade—at least, the best part of it—from the other, which is chiefly owing to the situation. For that Falmouth lying upon the sea, but within the entrance, ships of the greatest burthen come up to the very quays, and the whole Royal Navy might ride safely in the road; whereas the town of Truro lying far within, and at the mouth of two fresh rivers, is not navigable for vessels of above 150 tons or thereabouts.

Some have suggested that the original of Falmouth was the having so large a quay, and so good a depth of water at it. The merchants of Truro formerly used it for the place of lading and unlading their ships, as the merchants of Exeter did at Topsham; and this is the more probable in that, as above, the wharfage of those landing-places is still the property of the corporation of Truro.

But let this be as it will, the trade is now in a manner wholly gone to Falmouth, the trade at Truro being now chiefly (if not only) for the shipping off of block tin and copper ore, the latter being lately found in large quantities in some of the mountains between Truro and St. Michael's, and which is much improved since the several mills are erected at Bristol and other parts for the manufactures of battery ware, as it is called (brass), or which is made out of English copper, most of it duct in these parts—the ore itself ago being found very rich and good.

Falmouth is well built, has abundance of shipping belonging to it, is full of rich merchants, and has a flourishing and increasing trade. I say "increasing," because by the late setting up the English packets between this port and Lisbon, there is a new commerce between Portugal and this town carried on to a very great value.

It is true, part of this trade was founded in a clandestine commerce carried on by the said packets at Lisbon, where, being the king's ships, and claiming the privilege of not being searched or visited by the Custom House officers, they found means to carry off great quantities of British manufactures, which they sold on board to the Portuguese merchants, and they conveyed them on shore, as it is supposed, without paying custom.

But the Government there getting intelligence of it, and complaint being made in England also, where it was found to be very prejudicial to the fair merchant, that trade has been effectually stopped. But the Falmouth merchants, having by this means gotten a taste of the Portuguese trade, have maintained it ever since in ships of their own. These packets bring over such vast quantities of gold in specie, either in moidores (which is the Portugal coin) or in bars of gold, that I am very credibly informed the carrier from Falmouth brought by land from thence to London at one time, in the month of January, 1722, or near it, eighty thousand moidores in gold, which came from Lisbon in the packet-boats for account of the merchants at London, and that it was attended with a guard of twelve horsemen well armed, for which the said carrier had half per cent. for his hazard.

This is a specimen of the Portugal trade, and how considerable it is in itself, as well as how advantageous to England; but as that is not to the present case, I proceed. The Custom House for all the towns in this port, and the head collector, is established at this town, where the duties (including the other ports) is very considerable. Here is also a very great fishing for pilchards; and the merchants for Falmouth have the chief stroke in that gainful trade.

Truro is, however, a very considerable town, too. It stands up the water north and by east from Falmouth, in the utmost extended branch of the Avon, in the middle between the conflux of two rivers, which, though not of any long course, have a very good appearance for a port, and make it large wharf between them in the front of the town. And the water here makes a good port for small ships, though it be at the influx, but not for ships of burthen. This is the particular town where the Lord-Warden of the Stannaries always holds his famous Parliament of miners, and for stamping of tin. The town is well built, but shows that it has been much fuller, both of houses and inhabitants, than it is now; nor will it probably ever rise while the town of Falmouth stands where it does, and while the trade is settled in it as it is. There are at least three churches in it, but no Dissenters' meeting-house that I could hear of.

Tregony is upon the same water north-east from Falmouth—distance about fifteen miles from it—but is a town of very little trade; nor, indeed, have any of the towns, so far within the shore, notwithstanding the benefit of the water, any considerable trade but what is carried on under the merchants of Falmouth or Truro. The chief thing that is to be said of this town is that it sends members to Parliament, as does also Grampound, a market-town; and Burro', about four miles farther up the water. This place, indeed, has a claim to antiquity, and is an appendix to the Duchy of Cornwall, of which it holds at a fee farm rent and pays to the Prince of Wales as duke £10 11s. 1d. per annum. It has no parish church, but only a chapel-of-ease to an adjacent parish.

Penryn is up the same branch of the Avon as Falmouth, but stands four miles higher towards the west; yet ships come to it of as great a size as can come to Truro itself. It is a very pleasant, agreeable town, and for that reason has many merchants in it, who would perhaps otherwise live at Falmouth. The chief commerce of these towns, as to their sea-affairs, is the pilchards and Newfoundland fishing, which is very profitable to them all. It had formerly a conventual church, with a chantry and a religious house (a cell to Kirton); but they are all demolished, and scarce the ruins of them distinguishable enough to know one part from another.

Quitting Falmouth Haven from Penryn West, we came to Helston, about seven miles, and stands upon the little River Cober, which, however, admits the sea so into its bosom as to make a tolerable good harbour for ships a little below the town. It is the fifth town allowed for the coining tin, and several of the ships called tin-ships are laden here.

This town is large and populous, and has four spacious streets, a handsome church, and a good trade. This town also sends members to Parliament. Beyond this is a market-town, though of no resort for trade, called Market Jew. It lies, indeed, on the seaside, but has no harbour or safe road for shipping.

At Helford is a small but good harbour between Falmouth and this port, where many times the tin-ships go in to load for London; also here are a good number of fishing vessels for the pilchard trade, and abundance of skilful fishermen. It was from this town that in the great storm which happened November 27, 1703, a ship laden with tin was blown out to sea and driven to the Isle of Wight in seven hours, having on board only one man and two boys. The story is as follows:—

"The beginning of the storm there lay a ship laden with tin in Helford Haven, about two leagues and a half west of Falmouth. The tin was taken on board at a place called Guague Wharf, five or six miles up the river, and the vessel was come down to Helford in order to pursue her voyage to London.

"About eight o'clock in the evening the commander, whose name was Anthony Jenkins, went on board with his mate to see that everything was safe, and to give orders, but went both on shore again, leaving only a man and two boys on board, not apprehending any danger, they being in safe harbour. However, he ordered them that if it should blow hard they should carry out the small bower anchor, and so to moor the ship by two anchors, and then giving what other orders he thought to be needful, he went ashore, as above.

"About nine o'clock, the wind beginning to blow harder, they carried out the anchor, according to the master's order; but the wind increasing about ten, the ship began to drive, so they carried out their best bower, which, having a good new cable, brought the ship up. The storm still increasing, they let go the kedge anchor; so that they then rode by four anchors ahead, which were all they had.

"But between eleven and twelve o'clock the wind came about west and by south, and blew in so violent and terrible a manner that, though they rode under the lee of a high shore, yet the ship was driven from all her anchors, and about midnight drove quite out of the harbour (the opening of the harbour lying due east and west) into the open sea, the men having neither anchor or cable or boat to help themselves.

"In this dreadful condition (they driving, I say, out of the harbour) their first and chief care was to go clear of the rocks which lie on either side the harbour's mouth, and which they performed pretty well. Then, seeing no remedy, they consulted what to do next. They could carry no sail at first— no, not a knot; nor do anything but run away afore it. The only thing they had to think on was to keep her out at sea as far as they could, for fear of a point of land called the Dead Man's Head, which lies to the eastward of Falmouth Haven; and then, if they could escape the land, thought to run in for Plymouth next morning, so, if possible, to save their lives.

"In this frighted condition they drove away at a prodigious rate, having sometimes the bonnet of their foresail a little out, but the yard lowered almost to the deck—sometimes the ship almost under water, and sometimes above, keeping still in the offing, for fear of the land, till they might see daylight. But when the day broke they found they were to think no more of Plymouth, for they were far enough beyond it; and the first land they made was Peverel Point, being the southernmost land of the Isle of Purbeck, in Dorsetshire, and a little to the westward of the Isle of Wight; so that now they were in a terrible consternation, and driving still at a prodigious rate. By seven o'clock they found themselves broadside of the Isle of Wight.

"Here they consulted again what to do to save their lives. One of the boys was for running her into the Downs; but the man objected that, having no anchor or cable nor boat to go on shore with, and the storm blowing off shore in the Downs, they should be inevitably blown off and lost upon the unfortunate Goodwin—which, it seems, the man had been on once before and narrowly escaped.

"Now came the last consultation for their lives. The other of the boys said he had been in a certain creek in the Isle of Wight, where, between the rocks, he knew there was room to run the ship in, and at least to save their lives, and that he saw the place just that moment; so he desired the man to let him have the helm, and he would do his best and venture it. The man gave him the helm, and he stood directly in among the rocks, the people standing on the shore thinking they were mad, and that they would in a few minutes be dashed in a thousand pieces.

"But when they came nearer, and the people found they steered as if they knew the place, they made signals to them to direct them as well as they could, and the young bold fellow run her into a small cove, where she stuck fast, as it were, between the rocks on both sides, there being but just room enough for the breadth of the ship. The ship indeed, giving two or three knocks, staved and sunk, but the man and the two youths jumped ashore and were safe; and the lading, being tin, was afterwards secured.

"N.B.—The merchants very well rewarded the three sailors, especially the lad that ran her into that place."

Penzance is the farthest town of any note west, being 254 miles from London, and within about ten miles of the promontory called the Land's End; so that this promontory is from London 264 miles, or thereabouts. This town of Penzance is a place of good business, well built and populous, has a good trade, and a great many ships belonging to it, notwithstanding it is so remote. Here are also a great many good families of gentlemen, though in this utmost angle of the nation; and, which is yet more strange, the veins of lead, tin, and copper ore are said to be seen even to the utmost extent of land at low-water mark, and in the very sea—so rich, so valuable, a treasure is contained in these parts of Great Britain, though they are supposed to be so poor, because so very remote from London, which is the centre of our wealth.

Between this town and St. Burien, a town midway between it and the Land's End, stands a circle of great stones, not unlike those at Stonehenge, in Wiltshire, with one bigger than the rest in the middle. They stand about twelve feet asunder, but have no inscription; neither does tradition offer to leave any part of their history upon record, as whether it was a trophy or a monument of burial, or an altar for worship, or what else; so that all that can be learned of them is that here they are. The parish where they stand is called Boscawone, from whence the ancient and honourable family of Boscawen derive their names.

Near Penzance, but open to the sea, is that gulf they call Mount's Bay; named so from a high hill standing in the water, which they call St. Michael's Mount: the seamen call it only the Cornish Mount. It has been fortified, though the situation of it makes it so difficult of access that, like the Bass in Scotland, there needs no fortification; like the Bass, too, it was once made a prison for prisoners of State, but now it is wholly neglected. There is a very good road here for shipping, which makes the town of Penzance be a place of good resort.

A little up in the county towards the north-west is Godolchan, which though a hill, rather than a town, gives name to the noble and ancient family of Godolphin; and nearer on the northern coast is Royalton, which since the late Sydney Godolphin, Esq., a younger brother of the family, was created Earl of Godolphin, gave title of Lord to his eldest son, who was called Lord Royalton during the life of his father. This place also is infinitely rich in tin-mines.

I am now at my journey's end. As to the islands of Scilly, which lie beyond the Land's End, I shall say something of them presently. I must now return sur mes pas, as the French call it; though not literally so, for I shall not come back the same way I went. But as I have coasted the south shore to the Land's End, I shall come back by the north coast, and my observations in my return will furnish very well materials for another letter.

APPENDIX TO LAND'S END.

I have ended this account at the utmost extent of the island of Great Britain west, without visiting those excrescences of the island, as I think I may call them—viz., the rocks of Scilly; of which what is most famous is their infamy or reproach; namely, how many good ships are almost continually dashed in pieces there, and how many brave lives lost, in spite of the mariners' best skill, or the lighthouses' and other sea-marks' best notice.

These islands lie so in the middle between the two vast openings of the north and south narrow seas (or, as the sailors call them, the Bristol Channel, and The Channel—so called by way of eminence) that it cannot, or perhaps never will, be avoided but that several ships in the dark of the night and in stress of weather, may, by being out in their reckonings, or other unavoidable accidents, mistake; and if they do, they are sure, as the sailors call it, to run "bump ashore" upon Scilly, where they find no quarter among the breakers, but are beat to pieces without any possibility of escape.

One can hardly mention the Bishop and his Clerks, as they are called, or the rocks of Scilly, without letting fall a tear to the memory of Sir Cloudesley Shovel and all the gallant spirits that were with him, at one blow and without a moment's warning dashed into a state of immortality—the admiral, with three men-of-war, and all their men (running upon these rocks right afore the wind, and in a dark night) being lost there, and not a man saved. But all our annals and histories are full of this, so I need say no more.

They tell us of eleven sail of merchant-ships homeward bound, and richly laden from the southward, who had the like fate in the same place a great many years ago; and that some of them coming from Spain, and having a great quantity of bullion or pieces of eight on board, the money frequently drives on shore still, and that in good quantities, especially after stormy weather.

**82**

This may be the reason why, as we observed during our short stay here, several mornings after it had blown something hard in the night, the sands were covered with country people running to and fro to see if the sea had cast up anything of value. This the seamen call "going a-shoring;" and it seems they do often find good purchase. Sometimes also dead bodies are cast up here, the consequence of shipwrecks among those fatal rocks and islands; as also broken pieces of ships, casks, chests, and almost everything that will float or roll on shore by the surges of the sea.

Nor is it seldom that the voracious country people scuffle and fight about the right to what they find, and that in a desperate manner; so that this part of Cornwall may truly be said to be inhabited by a fierce and ravenous people. For they are so greedy, and eager for the prey, that they are charged with strange, bloody, and cruel dealings, even sometimes with one another; but especially with poor distressed seamen when they come on shore by force of a tempest, and seek help for their lives, and where they find the rooks themselves not more merciless than the people who range about them for their prey.

Here, also, as a farther testimony of the immense riches which have been lost at several times upon this coast, we found several engineers and projectors— some with one sort of diving engine, and some with another; some claiming such a wreck, and some such-and-such others; where they alleged they were assured there were great quantities of money; and strange unprecedented ways were used by them to come at it: some, I say, with one kind of engine, and some another; and though we thought several of them very strange impracticable methods, yet I was assured by the country people that they had done wonders with them under water, and that some of them had taken up things of great weight and in a great depth of water. Others had split open the wrecks they had found in a manner one would have thought not possible to be done so far under water, and had taken out things from the very holds of the ships. But we could not learn that they had come at any pieces of eight, which was the thing they seemed most to aim at and depend upon; at least, they had not found any great quantity, as they said they expected.

However, we left them as busy as we found them, and far from being discouraged; and if half the golden mountains, or silver mountains either, which they promise themselves should appear, they will be very well paid for their labour.

From the tops of the hills on this extremity of the land you may see out into that they call the Chops of the Channel, which, as it is the greatest inlet of commerce, and the most frequented by merchant-ships of any place in the world, so one seldom looks out to seaward but something new presents— that is to say, of ships passing or repassing, either on the great or lesser Channel.

Upon a former accidental journey into this part of the country, during the war with France, it was with a mixture of pleasure and horror that we saw from the hills at the Lizard, which is the southern-most point of this land, an obstinate fight between three French men-of-war and two English, with a privateer and three merchant-ships in their company. The English had the misfortune, not only to be fewer ships of war in number, but of less force; so that while the two biggest French ships engaged the English, the third in the meantime took the two merchant-ships and went off with them. As to the picaroon or privateer, she was able to do little in the matter, not daring to come so near the men-of-war as to take a broadside, which her thin sides would not have been able to bear, but would have sent her to the bottom at once; so that the English men-of-war had no assistance from her, nor could she prevent the taking the two merchant-ships. Yet we observed that the English captains managed their fight so well, and their seamen behaved so briskly, that in about three hours both the Frenchmen stood off, and, being sufficiently banged, let us see that they had no more stomach to fight; after which the English—having damage enough, too, no doubt—stood away to the eastward, as we supposed, to refit.

This point of the Lizard, which runs out to the southward, and the other promontory mentioned above, make the two angles—or horns, as they are called—from whence it is supposed this county received its first name of Cornwall, or, as Mr. Camden says, Cornubia in the Latin, and in the British "Kernaw," as running out in two vastly extended horns. And indeed it seems as if Nature had formed this situation for the direction of mariners, as foreknowing of what importance it should be, and how in future ages these seas should be thus thronged with merchant-ships, the protection of whose wealth, and the safety of the people navigating them, was so much her early care that she stretched out the land so very many ways, and extended the points and promontories so far and in so many different places into the sea, that the land might be more easily discovered at a due distance, which way soever the ships should come.

Nor is the Lizard Point less useful (though not so far west) than the other, which is more properly called the Land's End; but if we may credit our mariners, it is more frequently first discovered from the sea. For as our mariners, knowing by the soundings when they are in the mouth of the Channel, do then most naturally stand to the southward, to avoid mistaking the Channel, and to shun the Severn Sea or Bristol Channel, but still more to avoid running upon Scilly and the rocks about it, as is observed before—I say, as they carefully keep to the southward till they think they are fair with the Channel, and then stand to the northward again, or north-east, to make the land, this is the reason why the Lizard is, generally speaking, the first land they make, and not the Land's End.

Then having made the Lizard, they either (first) run in for Falmouth, which is the next port, if they are taken short with easterly winds, or are in want of provisions and refreshment, or have anything out of order, so that they care not to keep the sea; or (secondly) stand away for the Ram Head and Plymouth Sound; or (thirdly) keep an offing to run up the Channel.

So that the Lizard is the general guide, and of more use in these cases than the other point, and is therefore the land which the ships choose to make first; for then also they are sure that they are past Scilly and all the dangers of that part of the island.

Nature has fortified this part of the island of Britain in a strange manner, and so, as is worth a traveller's observation, as if she knew the force and violence of the mighty ocean which beats upon it; and which, indeed, if the land was not made firm in proportion, could not withstand, but would have been washed away long ago.

First, there are the islands of Scilly and the rocks about them; these are placed like out-works to resist the first assaults of this enemy, and so break the force of it, as the piles (or starlings, as they are called) are placed before the solid stonework of London Bridge to fence off the force either of the water or ice, or anything else that might be dangerous to the work.

Then there are a vast number of sunk rocks (so the seamen call them), besides such as are visible and above water, which gradually lessen the quantity of water that would otherwise lie with an infinite weight and force upon the land. It is observed that these rocks lie under water for a great way off into the sea on every side the said two horns or points of land, so breaking the force of the water, and, as above, lessening the weight of it.

But besides this the whole terra firma, or body of the land which makes this part of the isle of Britain, seems to be one solid rock, as if it was formed by Nature to resist the otherwise irresistible power of the ocean. And, indeed, if one was to observe with what fury the sea comes on sometimes against the shore here, especially at the Lizard Point, where there are but few, if any, out-works, as I call them, to resist it; how high the waves come rolling forward, storming on the neck of one another (particularly when the wind blows off sea), one would wonder that even the strongest rocks themselves should be able to resist and repel them. But, as I said, the country seems to be, as it were, one great body of stone, and prepared so on purpose.

And yet, as if all this was not enough, Nature has provided another strong fence, and that is, that these vast rocks are, as it were, cemented together by the solid and weighty ore of tin and copper, especially the last, which is plentifully found upon the very outmost edge of the land, and with which the stones may be said to be soldered together, lest the force of the sea should separate and disjoint them, and so break in upon these fortifications of the island to destroy its chief security.

This is certain—that there is a more than ordinary quantity of tin, copper, and lead also placed by the Great Director of Nature in these very remote angles (and, as I have said above, the ore is found upon the very surface of the rocks a good way into the sea); and that it does not only lie, as it were, upon or between the stones among the earth (which in that case might be washed from it by the sea), but that it is even blended or mixed in with the stones themselves, that the stones must be split into pieces to come at it. By this mixture the rocks are made infinitely weighty and solid, and thereby still the more qualified to repel the force of the sea.

Upon this remote part of the island we saw great numbers of that famous kind of crows which is known by the name of the Cornish cough or chough (so the country people call them). They are the same kind which are found in Switzerland among the Alps, and which Pliny pretended were peculiar to those mountains, and calls the pyrrhocorax. The body is black; the legs, feet, and bill of a deep yellow, almost to a red. I could not find that it was affected for any good quality it had, nor is the flesh good to eat, for it feeds much on fish and carrion; it is counted little better than a kite, for it is of ravenous quality, and is very mischievous. It will steal and carry away anything it finds about the house that is not too heavy, though not fit for its food—as knives, forks, spoons, and linen cloths, or whatever it can fly away with; sometimes they say it has stolen bits of firebrands, or lighted candles, and lodged them in the stacks of corn and the thatch of barns and houses, and set them on fire; but this I only had by oral tradition.

I might take up many sheets in describing the valuable curiosities of this little Chersonese or Neck Land, called the Land's End, in which there lies an immense treasure and many things worth notice (I mean, besides those to be found upon the surface), but I am too near the end of this letter. If I have opportunity I shall take notice of some part of what I omit here in my return by the northern shore of the county.

TWO LETTERS
FROM THE "JOURNEY THROUGH ENGLAND BY A GENTLEMAN."

Published in 1722, but not by Defoe.

BATH IN 1722.

Bath.

Sir,

The Bath lies very low, is but a small city, but very compact, and one can hardly imagine it could accommodate near the company that frequents it at least three parts of the year. I have been told of 8,000 families there at a time —some for the benefit of drinking its hot waters, others for bathing, and others for diversion and pleasure (of which, I must say, it affords more than any public place of that kind in Europe).

I told you in my former letters that Epsom and Tunbridge do not allow visiting (the companies there meet only on the walks); but here visits are received and returned, assemblies and balls are given, and parties at play in most houses every night, to which one Mr. Nash hath for many years contributed very much. This gentleman is by custom a sort of master of ceremonies of the place; he is not of any birth nor estate, but by a good address and assurance ingratiates himself into the good graces of the ladies and the best company in the place, and is director of all their parties of pleasure. He wears good clothes, is always affluent of money, plays very much, and whatever he may get in private, yet in public he always seems to lose. The town have been for many years so sensible of the service he does them that they ring the bells generally at his arrival in town, and, it is thought, pay him a yearly contribution for his support.

In the morning early the company of both sexes meet at the Pump (in a great hall enrailed), to drink the waters and saunter about till prayer-time, or divert themselves by looking on those that are bathing in the bath. Most of the company go to church in the morning in dishabille, and then go home to dress for the walks before dinner. The walks are behind the church, spacious and well shaded, planted round with shops filled with everything that contributes to pleasure, and at the end a noble room for gaming, from whence there are hanging-stairs to a pretty garden for everybody that pays for the time they stay, to walk in.

I have often wondered that the physicians of these places prescribe gaming to their patients, in order to keep their minds free from business and thought, that their waters on an undisturbed mind may have the greater effect, when indeed one cross-throw at play must sour a man's blood more than ten glasses of water will sweeten, especially for such great sums as they throw for every day at Bath.

The King and Queen's Baths, which have a communication with one another, are the baths which people of common rank go into promiscuously; and indeed everybody, except the first quality. The way of going into them is very comical: a chair with a couple of chairmen come to your bedside (lie in what storey you will), and there strip you, and give you their dress without your shift, and wrapping you up in blankets carry you to the bath.

When you enter the bath, the water seems very warm; and the heat much increases as you go into the Queen's Bath, where the great spring rises. On a column erected over the spring is an inscription of the first finder-out of these springs, in the following words: that "Bladud, the son of Lud, found them three hundred years before Christ." The smoke and slime of the waters, the promiscuous multitude of the people in the bath, with nothing but their heads and hands above water, with the height of the walls that environ the bath, gave me a lively idea of several pictures I had seen, of Angelo's in Italy of Purgatory, with heads and hands uplifted in the midst of smoke, just as they are here. After bathing, you are carried home in your chair, in the same manner you came.

The Cross Bath, which is used by the people of the first quality, was beautified and inclosed for the convenience of the late King James's queen, who after the priests and physicians had been at work to procure a male successor to the throne of Great Britain, the Sacrament exposed in all the Roman Catholic countries, and for that end a sanctified smock sent from the Virgin Mary at Loretto, the queen was ordered to go to Bath and prepare herself, and the king to make a progress through the western counties and join her there. On his arrival at Bath, the next day after his conjunction with the queen, the Earl of Melfort (then Secretary of State for Scotland) erected a fine prophetic monument in the middle of the Bath, as an everlasting monument of that conjunction. I call it "prophetic," because nine months after a Prince of Wales was born. This monument is still entire and handsome, only some of the inscriptions on the pillar were erased in King William's time. The angels attending the Holy Ghost as He descends, the Eucharist, the Pillar, and all the ornaments are of fine marble, and must have cost that earl a great deal of money. He was second son to Drummond, Earl of Perth, in North Britain; and was Deputy Governor of the Castle of Edinburgh when the Duke and Duchess of York came to Scotland, in King Charles the Second's time. He was a handsome gentleman, with a good address, and went into all the measures of that court, and at all their balls generally danced with the duchess; who, on their accession to the throne, sent for him up to London, made him Secretary of State for Scotland, created him Earl of Melfort, and Knight of the Order of St. Andrew. His elder brother was also made Chancellor and Governor of Scotland. And on King James's abdication, as the two brothers followed the king's fortunes, the Earl of Perth was made governor to the young prince; and Melfort was created a duke, had the Garter, and was a great man in France to his dying day.

There is another bath for lepers.

The cathedral church is small but well lighted. There are abundance of little monuments in it of people who come there for their health, but meet with their death.

These waters have a wonderful influence on barren ladies, who often prove with child even in their husbands' absence; who must not come near them till their bodies are prepared.

Everything looks gay and serene here; it is plentiful and cheap. Only the taverns do not much improve, for it is a place of universal sobriety. To be drunk at Bath is as scandalous as mad. Common women are not to be met with here so much as at Tunbridge and Epsom. Whether it is the distance from London, or that the gentlemen fly at the highest game, I cannot tell; besides, everything that passes here is known on the walks, and the characters of persons.

In three hours one arrives from Bath at Bristol, a large, opulent, and fine city; but, notwithstanding its nearness, by the different manners of the people seems to be another country. Instead of that politeness and gaiety which you see at Bath, here is nothing but hurry—carts driving along with merchandises, and people running about with cloudy looks and busy faces. When I came to the Exchange I was surprised to see it planted round with stone pillars, with broad boss-plates on them like sun-dials, and coats-of-arms with inscriptions on every plate.

They told me that these pillars were erected by eminent merchants for the benefit of writing and despatching their affairs on them, as on tables; and at 'Change time the merchants take each their stands by their pillars, that masters of ships and owners may know where to find them.

Coffee-houses and taverns lie round the 'Change, just as at London; and the Bristol milk, which is Spanish sherry (nowhere so good as here), is plentifully drunk.

The city of Bristol is situated much like Verona, in Italy. A river runs through almost the middle of it, on which there is a fine stone bridge. The quay may be made the finest, largest, and longest in the world by pulling down an old house or two. Behind the quay is a very noble square, as large as that of Soho in London, in which is kept the Custom House; and most of the eminent merchants who keep their coaches reside here. The cathedral is on the other side of the river, on the top of the hill, and is the meanest I have seen in England. But the square or green adjoining to it has several fine houses, and makes by its situation, in my opinion, much the pleasantest part of the town. There are some churches in the city finer than the cathedral, and your merchants have their little country-seats in the adjacent eminences; of which that of Mr. Southwell hath a very commanding prospect, both of the city, the River Severn, and the shipping that lies below.

There are hot springs near Bristol that are also very much frequented, and are reckoned to be better than the Bath for some distempers.

A traveller when he comes to the Bath must never fail of seeing Badminton, belonging to the Dukes of Beaufort; nor Longleat, belonging to my Lord Weymouth. They are both within a few miles of the Bath. King William, when he took Badminton in his way from Ireland, told the duke that he was not surprised at his not coming to court, having so sumptuous a palace to keep a court of his own in. And indeed the apartments are inferior to few royal palaces. The parks are large, and enclosed with a stone wall; and that duke, whom I described to you in my letter from Windsor, lived up to the grandeur of a sovereign prince. His grandson, who was also Knight of the Garter, made a great figure in the reign of Queen Anne. The family, which is a natural branch of the house of Lancaster, have always distinguished themselves of the Tory side. The present duke is under age.

Longleat, though an old seat, is very beautiful and large; and the gardens and avenue, being full-grown, are very beautiful and well kept. It cost the late Lord Weymouth a good revenue in hospitality to such strangers as came from Bath to see it.

The biggest and most regular house in England was built near Bristol by the late Lord Stawell; but it being judged by his heirs to be too big for the estate, they are pulling it down and selling the materials.

As the weather grows good, I shall proceed through South Wales to Chester, from whence you shall soon hear from me, who am without reserve, sir, your most humble, &c.

FROM CHESTER TO HOLYHEAD.

Chester.

Sir,

I crossed the Severn at the ferry of Ash, about ten miles above Bristol, and got to Monmouth to dinner through a rugged, indifferent country. It is a pitiful old town, and hath nothing remarkable in it; and from thence through a fat fertile country I got to the city of Hereford at night.

Hereford is the dirtiest old city I have seen in England, yet pretty large; the streets are irregular and the houses old, and its cathedral a reverend old pile, but not beautiful; the niches of the walls of the church are adorned with the figures of its bishops as big as the life, in a cumbent posture, with the year of their interments newly painted over. Some of them are in the twelve hundredth year of Christ. Here they drink nothing but cider, which is very cheap and very good; and the very hedges in the country are planted with apple-trees. About three miles from Hereford in my road to Ludlow I saw a fine old seat called Hampton Court, belonging to my Lord Coningsby. The plantations on rising grounds round it give an august splendour to the house, which consists of an oval court with suitable offices, not unlike an house belonging to the Duke of Somerset near London; and from thence in a few hours I arrived at Ludlow, the capital of South Wales, and where the Princes of Wales formerly, and since them the Presidents of Wales, kept their courts.

Ludlow is one of the neatest, clean, pretty towns in England. The street by which you enter the town is spacious, with handsome houses sash-windowed on each side, which leads you by an ascent to the castle on the left of the top of the hill, and the church on the right, from whence there runs also another handsome street. The castle hath a very commanding prospect of the adjacent country; the offices in the outer court are falling down, and a great part of the court is turned into a bowling-green; but the royal apartments in the castle, with some old velvet furniture and a sword of state, are still left. There is also a neat little chapel; but the vanity of the Welsh gentry when they were made councillors has spoiled it by adorning it with their names and arms, of which it is full.

A small expense would still make this castle a habitable and beautiful place, lying high, and overlooking a fine country; there is also a fine prospect from the churchyard, and the church is very neat. I saw abundance of pretty ladies here, and well dressed, who came from the adjacent counties, for the convenience and cheapness of boarding. Provisions of all sorts are extremely plentiful and cheap here, and very good company.

I stayed some days here, to make an excursion into South Wales and know a little of the manners of the country, as I design to do at Chester for North Wales. The gentry are very numerous, exceedingly civil to strangers, if you don't come to purchase and make your abode amongst them. They live much like Gascoynes—affecting their own language, valuing themselves much on the antiquity of their families, and are proud of making entertainments.

The Duke of Powis, of the name of Herbert, hath a noble seat near this town, but I was not at it; the family followed King James's fortunes to France, and I suppose the seat lies neglected. From Ludlow in a short day's riding through a champaign country I arrived at the town of Shrewsbury.

Shrewsbury stands upon an eminence, encircled by the Severn like a horse-shoe; the streets are large, and the houses well built. My Lord Newport, son to the Earl of Bradford, hath a handsome palace, with hanging gardens down to the river; as also Mr. Kinnaston, and some other gentlemen. There is a good town-house, and the most coffee-houses round it that ever I saw in any town; but when you come into them, they are but ale-houses (only they think that the name of coffee-house gives a better air). King Charles would have made them a city, but they chose rather to remain a corporation, as they are, for which they were called the "proud Salopians." There is a great deal of good company in this town, for the convenience of cheapness; and there are assemblies and balls for the young ladies once a week. The Earl of Bradford and several others have handsome seats near it; from hence I came to Wrexham, in Wales, a beautiful market-town; the church is the beautifullest country church in England, and surpasses some cathedrals. I counted fifty-two statues as big as the life in the steeple or tower, which is built after the manner of your Dutch steeples, and as high as any there. I was there on a market-day, and was particularly pleased to see the Welsh ladies come to market in their laced hats, their own hair hanging round their shoulders, and blue and scarlet cloaks like our Amazons—some of them with a greyhound in a string in their hands.

Whitchurch, near it, hath a fine church, built by the Earl of Bridgwater; and so to Chester, an ancient and large city, with a commanding castle. The city consists of four large streets, which make an exact cross, with the town-house and Exchange in the middle; but you don't walk the streets here, but in galleries up one pair of stairs, which keeps you from the rain in winter, and sun in summer; and the houses and shops, with gardens, go all off these galleries, which they call rows. The city is walled round, and the wall so firmly paved that it gives you an agreeable prospect of the country and river, as you walk upon it. The churches are very neat, and the cathedral an august old pile; there is an ancient monument of an Emperor of Germany, with assemblies every week. While I continued at Chester, I made an excursion into North Wales, and went into Denbigh, the capital of that country, where are the remains of a very great and old castle, as is also at Flint, the capital of Flintshire. These castles were the frontier garrisons of Wales before it came under the subjection of England. The country is mountainous, and full of iron and lead works; and here they begin to differ from the English both in language and dress.

From Flint, along the seaside, in three hours I arrived at the famous cold bath called St. Winifred's Well; and the town from thence called Holywell is a pretty large well-built village, in the middle of a grove, in a bottom between, two hills. The well is in the foot of one of the hills, and spouts out about the bigness of a barrel at once, with such force that it turns three or four mills before it falls into the sea. The well where you bathe is floored with stone surrounded with pillars, on which stands a neat little chapel dedicated to St. Winifred, but now turned into a Protestant school. However, to supply the loss of this chapel, the Roman Catholics have chapels erected almost in every inn for the devotion of the pilgrims that flock hither from all the Popish parts of England. The water, you may imagine, is very cold, coming from the bowels of an iron mountain, and never having met with the influence of the sun till it runs from the well.

The legend of St. Winifred is too long and ridiculous for a letter; I leave you to Dr. Fleetwood (when Bishop of St. Asaph) for its description. I will only tell you, in two words, that this St. Winifred was a beautiful damsel that lived on the top of the hill; that a prince of the country fell deeply in love with her; that coming one day when her parents were abroad, and she resisting his passion, turned into rage, and as she was flying from him cut off her head, which rolled down the hill with her body, and at the place where it stopped gushed out this well of water. But there was also a good hermit that lived at the bottom of the hill, who immediately claps her head to her body, and by the force of the water and his prayers she recovered, and lived to perform many miracles for many years after. They give you her printed litanies at the well. And I observed the Roman Catholics in their prayers, not with eyes lifted up to heaven, but intent upon the water, as if it were the real blood of St. Winifred that was to wash them clean from all their sins.

In every inn you meet with a priest, habited like country gentlemen, and very good companions. At the "Cross Keys," where I lodged, there was one that had been marked out to me, to whom I was particularly civil at supper; but finding by my conversation I was none of them, he drank and swore like a dragoon, on purpose, as I imagine, to disguise himself. From Holywell in two hours I came to a handsome seat of Sir John Conway's at Redland, and next day to Conway.

I do not know any place in Europe that would make a finer landscape in a picture than Conway at a mile's distance. It lies on the side of a hill, on the banks of an arm of the sea about the breadth of the Thames at London, and within two little miles of the sea, over which we ferry to go to the town.

The town is walled round, with thirty watch-towers at proper distances on the walls; and the castle with its towers, being very white, makes an august show at a distance, being surrounded with little hills on both sides of the bay or river, covered with wood. But when you cross the ferry and come into the town, there is nothing but poverty and misery. The castle is a heap of rubbish uncovered, and these towers on the walls only standing vestiges of what Wales was when they had a prince of their own.

They speak all Welsh here, and if a stranger should lose his way in this county of Carnarvon, it is ten to one if he meets with any one that has English enough to set him right. The people are also naturally very surly, and even if they understand English, if you ask them a question their answer is, "Dame Salsenach," or "I cannot speak Saxon or English." Their Bibles and prayer-books are all printed in Welsh in our character; so that an Englishman can read their language, although he doth not understand a word of it. It hath a great resemblance of the Bas-Bretons, but they retain the letter and character as well as language, as the Scots and Highlanders do.

They retain several Popish customs in North Wales, for on Sunday (after morning service) the whole parish go to football till the afternoon service begins, and then they go to the ale-house and play at all manner of games (which ale-house is often kept by the parson, for their livings are very small).

They have also offerings at funerals, which is one of the greatest perquisites the parson hath. When the body is deposited in the church during the service for the dead, every person invited to the burial lays a piece of money upon the altar to defray the dead person's charges to the other world, which, after the ceremony is over, the parson puts in his pocket. From Conway, through the mountainous country of Carnarvon, I passed the famous mountain of Penmaen-Mawr, so dreadfully related by passengers travelling to Ireland. It is a road cut out of the side of the rock, seven feet wide; the sea lies perpendicularly down, about forty fathoms on one side, and the mountain is about the same height above it on the other side. It looks dismal, but not at all dangerous, for there is now a wall breast-high along the precipice. However, there is an ale-house at the bottom of the hill on the other side, with this inscription, "Now your fright is over, take a dram." From hence I proceeded to a little town called Bangor, where there is a cathedral such as may be expected in Wales; and from thence to Carnarvon, the capital of the county. Here are the vestiges of a large old castle, where one of the Henrys, King of England, was born; as was another at Monmouth, in South Wales. For the Welsh were so hard to be reconciled to their union with England at first, it was thought policy to send our queens to lie-in there, to make our princes Welshmen born, and that way ingratiate the inhabitants to their subjection to a prince born in their own country. And for that reason our kings to this day wear a leek (the badge of Wales) on St. David's Day, the patron of this country; as they do the Order of the Thistle on St. Andrew's Day, the patron of Scotland.

Carnarvon is a pretty little town, situated in the bottom of a bay, and might be a place of good trade, if the country afforded a consumption.

The sea flows quite round from Bangor to Carnarvon Bay, which separates Anglesea from the rest of Wales, and makes it an island. Beaumaris, the capital of the island, hath been a flourishing town; there are still two very good streets, and the remains of a very large castle. The Lord Bulkeley hath a noble ancient seat planted with trees on the side of the hill above the town, from whence one hath a fine prospect of the bay and adjacent country; the church is very handsome, and there are some fine ancient monuments of that family and some Knights Templars in it. The family of Bulkeley keep in their family a large silver goblet, with which they entertain their friends, with an inscription round relating to the royal family when in distress, which is often remembered by the neighbouring gentry, whose affections run very much that way all over Wales.

I went from hence to Glengauny, the ancient residence of Owen Tudor, but now belongs to the Bulkeleys, and to be sold. It is a good old house, and I believe never was larger. There is a vulgar error in this country that Owen Tudor was married to a Queen of England, and that the house of York took that surname from him; whereas the Queen of England that was married to him was a daughter of the King of France and dowager of England, and had no relation to the Crown; he had indeed two daughters by her, that were married into English noble families—to one of which Henry VII. was related. But Owen Tudor was neither of the blood of the Princes of Wales himself, nor gave descent to that of the English. He was a private gentleman, of about £3,000 a year, who came to seek his fortune at the English court, and the queen fell in love with him.

I was invited to a cock-match some miles from Glengauny, where were above forty gentlemen, most of them of the names of Owen, Parry, and Griffith; they fought near twenty battles, and every battle a cock was killed. Their cocks are doubtless the finest in the world; and the gentlemen, after they were a little heated with liquor, were as warm as their cocks. A great deal of bustle and noise grew by degrees after dinner was over; but their scolding was all in Welsh, and civilities in English. We had a very great dinner; and the house (called The College) where we dined was built very comically; it is four storeys high, built on the side of a hill, and the stable is in the garret. There is a broad stone staircase on the outside of the house, by which you enter into the several apartments. The kitchen is at the bottom of the hill, a bedchamber above that, the parlour (where we dined) is the third storey, and on the top of the hill is the stable.

From hence I stepped over to Holyhead, where the packet-boats arrive from Ireland. It is a straggling, confused heap of thatched houses built on rocks; yet within doors there are in several of them very good accommodation for passengers, both in lodging and diet.

The packet-boats from Dublin arrive thrice a week, and are larger than those to Holland and France, fitted with all conveniences for passengers; and indeed St. George's Channel requires large ships in winter, the wind being generally very boisterous in these narrow seas.

On my return to Chester I passed over the mountain called Penmaen Ross, where I saw plainly a part of Ireland, Scotland, England, and the Isle of Man all at once. The End.

98

Www.freerivercommunity.com

Daniel Defoe (1660 – 24 April 1731)
Henry Morley (15 September 1822 – 1894)

13338836R00057

Printed in Great Britain
by Amazon.co.uk, Ltd.,
Marston Gate.